Three Years in Ethiopia

Three Years in Ethiopia

How a Civil War and Epidemics Led Me to my Daughter

Cornelia E. Davis

KonjitPublications

The author has made every effort to ensure that the information in this book is correct. The events, locales, and conversations are based on the author's memories of them, and any unwitting errors that may appear in the book are the author's own. Some names and identifying details have been changed to protect the privacy of individuals.

Copyright © 2019 by Cornelia E. Davis.
All rights reserved. No part of this publication may be reproduced, distributed, or transmitted in any form or by any means, including photocopying, recording, or other electronic or mechanical methods, without the prior written permission of the author, except in the case of brief quotations embodied in critical reviews and certain other noncommercial uses permitted by copyright law.

Published by KonjitPublications
Laredo, Texas

Library of Congress Control Number: 2019900196

Publisher's Cataloging-In-Publication Data
(Prepared by The Donohue Group, Inc.)
Names: Davis, Cornelia E., author.
Title: Three years in Ethiopia : how a civil war and epidemics led me to my daughter / Cornelia E. Davis.
Description: Laredo, Texas : KonjitPublications, [2019]
Identifiers: ISBN 9780999303443 | ISBN 9780999303450 (ebook)
Subjects: LCSH: Davis, Cornelia E. | Women physicians--United States--Biography. | Medical assistance--Ethiopia. | Orphans--Ethiopia. | Meningitis--Ethiopia--Prevention. | Mothers and daughters--Ethiopia. | LCGFT: Autobiographies.
Classification: LCC R154.D277 A3 2019 (print) | LCC R154.D277 (ebook) | DDC 610.92--dc23

Epigraph taken from *Remember When* by Judith McNaught, published in 1996 by Simon & Schuster, Inc.

Cover photo by: Mark Thomas

Book design by: Christy Collins, Constellation Book Services

Every effort has been made to fulfill requirements with regard to reproducing copyright material. The author will be glad to rectify any omissions at the earliest opportunity.

This book is dedicated to my daughter, Romene.

There will be a few times in your life when all your instincts will tell you to do something, something that defies logic, upsets your plans, and may seem crazy to others. When that happens, just do it. Listen to your instincts and ignore everything else. Ignore logic, ignore the odds, ignore the complications, and just go for it!
— Judith McNaught

Contents

Acknowledgments	ix
1. Destiny	1
2. Addis Ababa	5
3. Arrival	10
4. Orientation	15
5. Field Trip	18
6. Disease Committee	25
7. Outbreak	30
8. Festivities	37
9. Addis Routine	40
10. Fingerprints	44
11. Refugee Camp	53
12. US Staff Depart	56
13. Uganda	62
14. Acting Director	68
15. A House with a View	72
16. Mengistu Flees	74
17. Statue Toppled	77
18. UN Evacuation	82
19. Rebels Capture Asmara	87
20. Call Sign WHISKEY	89
21. Emergency	93
22. The Rebels	100
23. Debre Zeit	107

25. House on Fire	115
26. Supplies Needed	119
27. Back to Hilton	126
28. Appeal	133
29. Black Lion Hospital	141
30. Waiting to Exhale	145
31. Ordered to Depart	152
32. A Favor	157
33. Whirlwind	165
34. The Mountains	169
35. Adoption	173
36. Return to Normal	178
37. Another Outbreak	187
38. Bonding	192
39. New Citizen	198
40. The Next Chapter	201
41. Leaving	205
42. The End	207
43. Postscript	213

Acknowledgments

Writing a memoir is always a little tricky. Your memory starts to fade as the years pass. But I was lucky to have a "compatriot in crime" who lived and worked along side me in Addis Ababa during those fateful three years. Monica Wernette worked in HIV/AIDS in the country office of the World Health Organization (WHO) in Ethiopia. She welcomed me, provided orientation, gave me useful tips so I could avoid the mistakes she made, supported me when my house was destroyed by an explosion of a underground ammunitions depot. She made the darkest moments survivable. Monica knew how to live in the moment. She provided invaluable "fact checking" in reading this memoir to make sure I remembered things correctly!

And many thanks go to my Editor, Lisa Carter of Intralingo. She kept the book focused and prevented me from going off in tangents. Lisa blocked me from falling into easy clichés and constantly raised probing questions. "Your readers will want to know this," she said. *But maybe I didn't want to tell all.*

And thank you Mark Thomas for capturing that "Mushroom Cloud" photo of the explosion and is the background of the book cover. He was the UNICEF photographer who was looking in the right place at the right time on that fateful morning. As I was the closest UN staff person to the explosion he gifted me an enlarged color photo of the moment. The photograph hangs in my study to constantly remind me: "to live as if you were to die tomorrow."

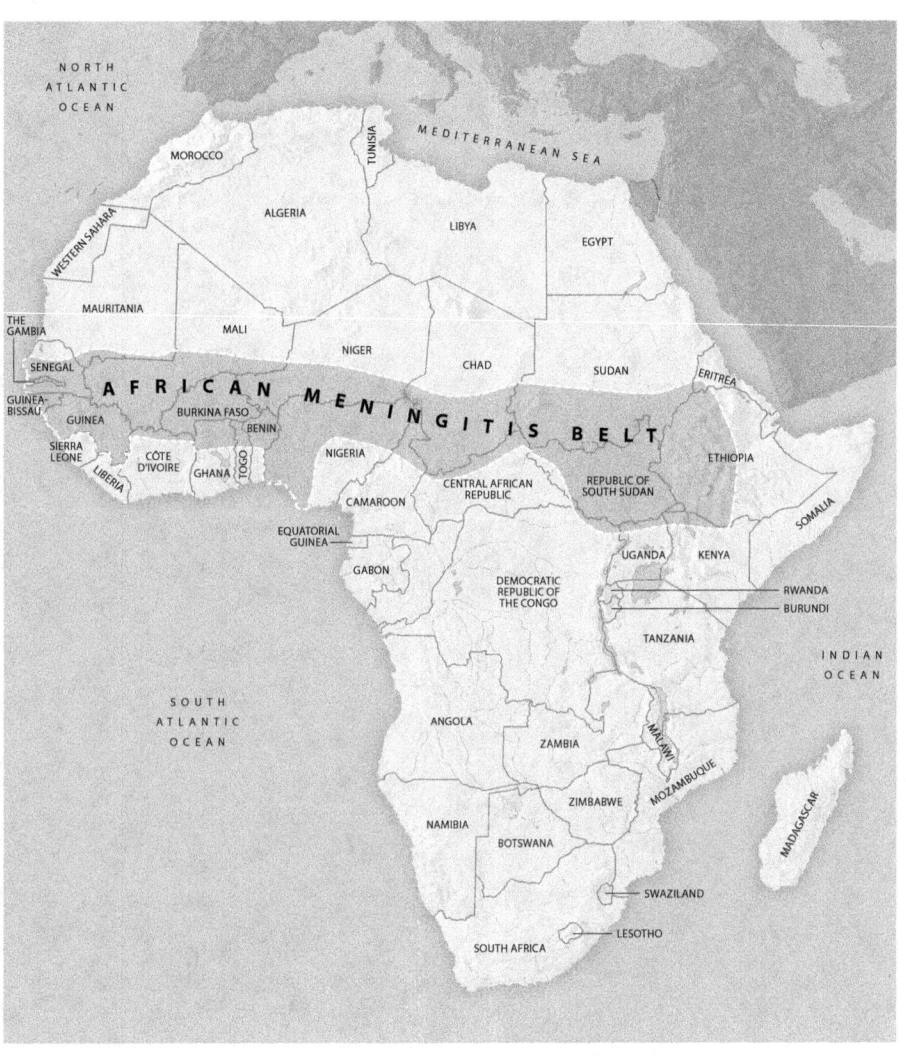

Chapter 1

Destiny

Destiny. Something about the word grates and leaves me unsettled. It alludes to a past but no history, to a future but no present. It is nonnegotiable, predestined. However you want to define it, destiny cannot be controlled, modified, prevented, or bribed. Let me be perfectly clear. I don't believe in destiny. I believe you determine your life through the choices you make and the course of actions you undertake. And yet, I have placed a lot of my trust over the years in something called *intuition*.

A beam of light flashed through the airplane window and jolted me from an uneasy sleep. I was on Ethiopian Airlines heading for Addis Ababa on vacation. I thought I deserved some respite from my United Nations Children's Fund (UNICEF) position as Primary Health Care Advisor in Dakar, Senegal. It was October 1989, and I was working to increase national and state childhood vaccination levels from a dismal current level of 40 percent to the goal of 80 percent before 1990.

This trip would finally put to rest a question that had bedeviled me since my graduate school days at the University of California, Berkeley campus. Foreign graduate students from

Ethiopia had regularly approached me while I was walking on campus or eating in the cafeteria. The first time it happened, I was grabbing a quick sandwich when a tall, dark, thin, handsome guy rushed up to me jabbering in a language I had never heard.

"*Tena yistilign*," he shouted, but seeing my stunned look, he quickly recovered and said, "Oh, sorry, I thought you were Ethiopian!"

"No, I'm American, from California," I said with pride.

He smiled and rushed off.

I didn't think much about it until it happened the third time. Why did these students think I was a foreigner? I couldn't "Google" anything then, in 1967 and 1968, and the family set of the Encyclopedia Britannica was in my parents' home gathering dust. I headed to the library and looked up Ethiopia. The country came across as intriguing, even exotic. This was the only African country during the nineteenth century that successfully resisted a European colonial power, retaining its sovereignty, and the only African country with its own script (Ge'ez). Ethiopia was famous for many things: the rock-hewn churches of Lalibela, the source of the Blue Nile, and the place where coffee beans were first discovered. It was also known for its beautiful women. These were all laudable facts, yet it still rankled me at the time that these Ethiopian students thought I was African and not an American.

The next time my identity was mistaken was years later, in 1976. I was sitting in the Taj Mahal Hotel bar in Bombay (now Mumbai), India. I was working on smallpox eradication, and the quickest way for me to get to Gujarat State, which was situated next door to Rajasthan State where I was posted, was to fly via Bombay. The Ethiopian Airlines crew had spied me, descended on the bar, and immediately started talking in Amharic. They still supplied me with a couple of free drinks even after I told them I wasn't Ethiopian.

So now, in 1989, I would be arriving in Addis Ababa and would soon be able to answer the question: Do I really look Ethiopian? I saw the airline flight attendants eyeing me and talking among themselves.

The drink carts were in the aisle, and soon one of the cabin crew came up to me and spoke in Amharic. She immediately noticed my quizzical look and said, "Sorry, we all thought you were an Ethiopian returning for a visit!"

I smiled and said, "No, I'm American, but Ethiopians in the States also think that, so I'm used to it. This will be my first time in Addis and I'm looking forward to it." I was looking forward to the visit, but I was nervous about the real reason I was coming to Addis.

The rest of the flight was uneventful.

Four hours later, the pilot came on the speaker and announced, "We are on our approach to Bole Airport in Addis Ababa, Ethiopia, and will be landing in twenty minutes. Please fasten your seat belts."

There were not many foreigners on the plane, so I was soon at the front of the immigration line for those with international passports. The officer signaled me to come forward. I smiled and placed my US passport on the counter. The officer picked up the passport and turned to the photo page. He glanced at me. He then flicked through the pages, seeing where I had been. He picked up the visa stamp and then hesitated. He said, "You really are Ethiopian, right?"

I responded, "Well, no. This is a US passport. I'm American."

He hesitated once again, and said, "But your parents are Ethiopian?"

"No, they are American."

He then put the entry approval stamp down and looked at me once more and said slightly louder, "But your grandparents are Ethiopian, right?" Now I started getting worried. Clearly he wanted me to admit to Ethiopian ancestry. I wasn't sure if he would stamp approval in my passport.

So I said, "Yes, they were!"

And then he smiled and picked up the stamp. "Welcome to Ethiopia!"

In an airport taxi speeding in a rather haphazard fashion to the Hilton Hotel, I pondered my real reason for being there. Ostensibly, I was here to "find my Ethiopian roots." But I actually was on a stealth mission. I was seriously considering applying for a posting with the World Health Organization (WHO) in Ethiopia, and I wanted to check out the real situation in the country. Some kind of unrest had erupted in the North. I also had another, parallel objective. I was thinking of adopting a child from Ethiopia and it was difficult to find out the government's criteria for adoption on the Internet. So I thought I'd combine a vacation with a fact-finding mission. I had the name of someone in the Ministry of Labour and Social Welfare, and my plan was to drop in to get the needed information and then go off to do the tourism thing. My intuition was telling me that Ethiopia might offer an easier route to adoption than the US.

Chapter 2

Addis Ababa
— 1989 —

In 1989, the only feasible way to get around in Addis Ababa as a foreigner was to hire a Hilton car and driver. And if you wanted to go on tour you were required to use the state-run Ethiopian Tourism Commission (ETC) to obtain the necessary permits. The Commission determined your travel schedule and booked your up-country lodges and hotels. Conveniently, the Hilton Hotel had an ETC office in situ. So I made contact right after breakfast to tell them when and where I wanted to travel. The nice lady said she would get right on it and told me to return in a few hours to confirm scheduling and activities.

I then went straight to the concierge to arrange a car and driver to head to the Ministry of Labour and Social Welfare (MLSW). If I was trying to blend in as a typical Ethiopian, my cover was blown. The car was a caramel-colored Mercedes sedan with a uniformed driver. The typical Ethiopian walked to their destination or piled into a taxi that held four to six people. The driver helped me locate the office of an *Ato* (Mr.) Werkesentayhu. I knocked on the door and entered.

"Good morning, Mr. Werkesentayhu," I said. "My name is Dr. Connie Davis. I'm sorry to just come barging in, but I work for UNICEF in Senegal, and I'm here on a short visit. I wanted to find out about adoption."

He looked up from some documents, smiled, and said, "Good morning, please have a seat." He indicated a chair in front of his desk.

His office was small and spartan, with sunlight streaming in from a window.

"I tried to find out about the government's criteria for foreigners wishing to adopt, but I couldn't find much information. So I thought I would drop in and pick up some informational brochures," I said.

"We don't have any," he said with a wry smile. And then he launched into what seemed like an oft-repeated summary of the Ethiopian government's position on adoption. In the Ethiopian context, adoptions did occur among relatives. Let's say your brother died and he had a small infant. An older brother or another blood relative might take the child into his home to raise. However, in the Ethiopian culture, families didn't normally adopt a child with no blood ties. And so children who were true orphans, with no known living relatives, were placed in orphanages. He stressed that Ethiopia was not like some Latin American countries that appeared to be facilitating the export of babies. Ethiopia preferred that orphans grew up in Ethiopia, knowing that they were Ethiopians. At the same time, the state recognized that living in an orphanage could never replace a loving family. So Ethiopia did allow a few international adoptions.

Then I asked my burning question. "Does Ethiopia allow single women to adopt?"

"Yes, if they meet the other criteria," said Werkesentayhu.

I continued along the same line of questioning. "Can single women adopt an infant?"

"Of course," he responded.

And then I asked one final question. "Are there any age restrictions?"

"Well, you should be under fifty years of age and able to financially support the child." Werke looked at me and smiled. "Since you work for the United Nations, I'm sure you can pass the financial qualifications."

We continued talking in a lighter manner. I told him I was considering taking a post with the WHO in Addis Ababa and if I did, then for sure he would see me again. Werkesentayhu mentioned that he had a conference coming up in Senegal in a few months. I reached in my purse and took out my business card and handed it to him.

"If you come to Dakar, please give me a ring. I'd like to invite you to dinner," I said.

"I will certainly look you up if I have that opportunity," replied Werke.

I started to get up to leave but hesitated. "So, if Ethiopia doesn't do a lot of international adoptions, what country sends in the most applications?"

He stood up and said, "Follow me!"

And then he took me out in the hallway and halted before a six-by-four-foot board nailed on the wall, full of photos of happy parents with their adopted children.

"Most adoptee parents are from Scandinavian countries."

"Who would have thought?" I said. "Do many Americans adopt?"

He looked at me. "Since I've been working here the last ten years, only a handful."

And so we said goodbye.

I was practically skipping out the door! Who would have thought Ethiopia had less prejudice against "older, single moms" than the United States! Not that I considered myself "old" at forty-three years. I had researched domestic adoptions, and the private agencies I investigated were quite blunt that an older, single woman would not get an infant. Infants were in short supply. If a single woman wanted to adopt, she should be ready to take an older child and one with disabilities. But I wanted an infant, and so the adoption issue was put on the backburner.

I was so happy "it was as if I had won the lottery!" I raced back to the Hilton to arrange my tour. Now I could relax and enjoy the sights. Two memories remain etched in my mind from my first visit to Ethiopia. One memory was that of the thundering cascades of the Blue Nile Falls, which required a short but steep hike through jungle to the edge of the gorge. The roar of the Falls was overwhelming, and you could barely talk over it. The spray from the falls was like a gentle rain covering your face and *shamma* (shawl), cooling you down from the exertion of the hike. It was mesmerizing and drew me closer to the precipice. It was some time before I remembered to take photos. I could imagine what those first explorers felt on seeing it for the first time.

The other memory was one of eating in a traditional restaurant on a *mesob* (a small round table woven like a basket) eating *injera* (the national pancake-like crepe that is used to scoop up the *wat*—meat and vegetables). Ethiopian food is extremely spicy, but it was washed down with *tej* (the traditional honey wine) and Ethiopian beer. What topped it off were the traditional dances and songs from different regions of Ethiopia. Especially striking was the dance where the men and women shake their shoulders vigorously and, I thought, provocatively. The dancers did not let me sit comfortably and observe, but came to my table to drag me to the dance floor to learn the seductive steps.

The traditional food and the dances cast a certain ambiance that would accompany me throughout my introductory excursion through Ethiopia, especially my visit to Gonder to see Emperor Fasilidas's Palace, the famous winged angels with their huge mahogany-colored eyes in Debre Birhan Selassie Church, and the Falashas. I thought of the Falashas as the Lost Tribe of Israel, who claimed they were Black Jews. At the time, I didn't know the term Falasha (wanderer, homeless) was actually a derogatory name given to them by the Christian community and they were persecuted through the ages because they would not accept Christianity. They called themselves Bete Isra'el, and at the time I visited them they lived a very marginal life subsisting on selling their pottery and blacksmithing. I couldn't know then that I would encounter the Falashas and an angel with huge dark eyes, on a later occasion in Ethiopia.

Chapter 3

Arrival
— 1990 —

I peered out of my window from the top floor of the Ghion Hotel one early foggy October morning in 1990. In the street below, three Ethiopian women were hunched over at almost a ninety-degree angle, due to the towering load of firewood on their backs. It was held in place by a thick band of rope that went across their foreheads and then around the load of wood. I couldn't see their faces, as they were bent over, but I could see the wisps of warm exhaled air as it met the cold mountain wind. Addis Ababa has an elevation of 7,726 feet and is ranked as the fourth-highest capital in the world. I had arrived to take up my post as Medical Epidemiologist at the WHO PanAfrican Emergency Preparedness and Response Centre. Welcome to Ethiopia!

So I headed off to the office. The first week in settling into any new post was filling out forms. And almost immediately I recognized that this country was vastly different from any of my previous posts. For starters, UN employees are given a housing allowance and, normally, head out to look for private lodging. But in Addis we had to fill out a form and apply to be placed on a waiting list for lodgings. The sooner I got my name on the official list from my organization, the faster I got my accommodations. As a single person, I would only be given a one-bedroom apartment, and not one of my choosing. Ostensibly, the official reason for assigning lodging was that there were more "official" personnel than adequate housing available. And the Provisional Military Government of Socialist Ethiopia, commonly referred to as the DERG, needed to oversee this function. They wanted to ensure that foreigners could not rent privately from the former landowner class and that no foreign currency (especially, USD) went into the hands of private citizens.

After the overthrow of the Emperor Haile Selassie in 1974, and the abrupt move of the country to Communism, a *Proclamation on Private Property* was issued on February 26, 1975. This proclamation abolished all private tenancy arrangements and nationalized all rural land. Subsequently, all urban land was nationalized to the lowest level—the *kebele*. In effect, the nationalization of all land abolished the economic basis of the landowner class. The former landowner class got to retain one house per family, but the government seized any other houses or land. Once the government seized control, revenue went directly to the regime. New arrivals to the capital would be placed into available lodgings. Right away, I could see how this would affect me. I was only entitled to a one-bedroom apartment but if I wanted to adopt, eventually I would need a larger residence. This would necessitate explaining my personal plans immediately, which I was reluctant to do at that moment.

UN personnel were also required to open a bank account in the capital, and a certain proportion of their salary was placed in the national bank. Since the government ranked one Ethiopian birr on a par with one USD, the official exchange rate made it exceedingly expensive to live in Ethiopia. I heard through the grapevine that on the black market one USD was worth ten birr! If a cappuccino cost 1.50 birr, if I used the official rate I paid the equivalent of 1.50 USD. Yet if I exchanged money on the black market, I only paid fifteen cents USD. It was quickly becoming clear this was an authoritarian government.

Now I understood why I was in the Ghion Hotel, which was government owned. It would be my abode probably for six to eight months! Well, at least I had lucked out on an apartment on the top floor with a view and a fireplace. True, I would have to pay for firewood, but it would provide a certain ambiance to the quarters. The WHO vehicle would pick me up daily and return me to the hotel. The WHO Emergency Preparedness and Response (EPR) Centre was a relatively new creation and was building up staff. The other staff working in the Preparedness Unit with me were a Finnish woman, who worked on Technological Disasters, and an Italian professional, who was the geographic information system (GIS) consultant. A Burmese doctor (Burma's name changed to Myanmar in 1989, but the name had not caught on yet) worked on humanitarian emergencies.

I'm not sure where I first met Monica Wernette in Ethiopia. It was probably in the WHO country office as I was returning what seemed like an unending number of administrative forms.

"Connie, what are you doing in Addis?" Monica said.

I stared at her, trying desperately to place where I had met this tall blonde woman with an infectious grin.

"Don't you remember, we met in Malawi at the Centers for Disease Control/Atlanta annual project meeting. You were stationed in Côte d'Ivoire, and I was a Public Health Officer in the Congo."

"Oh, right!" I declared. "How long have you been in Addis?"

"It's been a year and a half already," she said. "I'm working in the WHO country office on HIV/AIDS."

"And yours truly is posted in the WHO/EPR Centre," I offered.

"Come to my apartment for dinner tonight. I'll pick you up and give you the lowdown on things."

Monica turned out to be a real godsend for me. She knew how the bureaucracy worked and, more importantly, how to get it to work in your favor. She seemed to know everyone, and she was known for throwing amazing parties at her place to celebrate one thing or another. As I settled into her digs at Arat Kilo, an area of the city close to the American Embassy, with a glass of beer in my hand, I asked about life in Ethiopia. I told her I had to go to Brazzaville next week to check in with the WHO Regional Office for Africa (AFRO) and go for orientation. I would be working primarily on meningococcal meningitis, and my job would also take me outside Ethiopia to assist in preparedness and response activities in countries in the "meningitis belt" of sub-Saharan Africa.

"You're lucky, Connie. You get to periodically leave Addis and pass through Nairobi. You can pick up items that are impossible to find here. You'll also have access to dollars!"

Monica proceeded to explain the civil war in northern Ethiopia and how it would impact me. Several rebel groups in the North in the provinces of Eritrea and Tigray wanted to secede from Ethiopia. They had been fighting this obscure war for years but in the last year had grown more powerful and were winning more battles. Basically, in Ethiopia currently, I could travel by road or plane to the south to Awasa, to the east to Harar, and to the west to Gambela. But I wouldn't be going to the north anytime soon—to the Blue Nile Falls, Lalibela, or Gonder.

Monica gave me one more tip. "If you plan to be in Brazzaville for the weekend, be sure and take the ferry to Kinshasa. Kinshasa is known for its open-air restaurants and live bands. They roll the sidewalks up at five o'clock in Brazzaville!"

Chapter 4

Orientation

Off I went to spend a week at WHO/AFRO, meeting the epidemiologists working on communicable diseases in other African countries. I assumed the regional office would provide not only technical guidance, but also additional supplies such as vaccines and antibiotics to control epidemics in the concerned countries. I was looking forward to discussing the approach to preparedness training and how to encourage countries to prepare a preparedness and response plan for meningococcal meningitis, given that outcomes are usually good if cases are rapidly and appropriately treated.

On the African continent, epidemic meningitis caused by *Group A meningococcus* had been known to occur for a long time. It was first reported from the west coast of Africa by G. William in 1909 and has occurred regularly from then onwards, even though it is infrequent in developed countries with a temperate climate. The African meningitis belt extended from Ethiopia in the east to Senegal in the west. In this area, sporadic infections occurred in seasonal, annual cycles while large-scale epidemics occurred at greater intervals with irregular patterns (every eight to twelve years). In 1989, Ethiopia had an unprecedented outbreak. That one year in Ethiopia accounted for nearly 20 percent of all cases for the entire belt over a twenty-year period.

Large-scale epidemics caused untold suffering, increased morbidity (illness) and mortality, and had a destabilizing effect on national economies. Although it was impossible to precisely predict when these epidemics might occur, WHO thought the next large-scale outbreaks would occur in 1990 or close to that year. Donor countries such as the US, Italy, Denmark, Norway, and Sweden were prepared to provide resources to try to prevent and/or control the outbreaks. And this—planning how to use those resources—is how I was involved.

One of the tasks of the newly created PanAfrican WHO/EPR Centre was to assist countries to prepare emergency, preparedness, and response plans to respond rapidly to control the meningitis outbreaks. I was disconcerted to learn that initially I was the only epidemiologist who would be working on meningitis in the region. The WHO/EPR Centre was tasked with developing guidelines for preventing and controlling meningitis, and for responding to outbreaks. Once the manuals were developed, they could be used as templates to develop individual country plans for the control of meningitis. I would start to develop plans in two countries (Ethiopia and Uganda), but I was also charged with responding to other outbreaks if countries requested emergency assistance. Since I was working with a communicable disease, I might also be requested to respond to cholera and yellow fever outbreaks. I suppose AFRO didn't want me sitting around with time on my hands in case there were no meningitis cases! I was more concerned that I was the only epidemiologist working on meningitis in Africa and I would be overwhelmed if more than one country had outbreaks at the same time.

My week of training in Brazzaville sped by quickly. I respected the usual protocol and met the WHO regional director and—most importantly—Administration and Finance departments who would need to approve and fund my travel to countries outside my project area. While I was in Congo/Brazzaville, the lingua franca was French. Thank goodness I didn't have to write my reports in French, since I was based in an English-speaking country. It soon became abundantly clear that I would need to convince the Ethiopian Ministry of Health to convoke a committee to develop this emergency, preparedness, and response plan on meningitis. The plan needed to be a collaborative effort and felt to be important by the country, otherwise the probability of it ever being developed and implemented was about as likely as me being able to outrun an Ethiopian Nile crocodile.

Chapter 5

Field Trip

I arrived back in Addis and requested a meeting with the Minister of Health to explain the recommended way forward. Ethiopia would develop the guidelines in a manual and a plan to control meningitis, which could then be used as a template by other countries in the meningitis belt. He promised to convene a committee within a week, which would work with me in developing the guidelines. Great, I thought! Everything's going according to plan.

"So, Dr. Davis," the Minister said before leaving. "You might like to visit Sidamo province. They're currently experiencing several cases of meningitis, and it would give you a clearer picture of how meningitis is currently handled in Ethiopia."

I smiled and said, "Good idea." That knowledge would come in handy in developing the guidelines, in laying down precisely how meningitis should be treated. And this would be a great opportunity to see another region of Ethiopia by road. I always enjoyed going "to the field" in other countries. Since I was traveling in-country, the EPR Centre could handle the logistics.

As I headed towards the WHO Administrative office, Dr. Roma—my colleague in charge of humanitarian activities—

cautioned, "Be sure you know what time you'll be leaving!" Right, Ethiopia had its own system for telling time. And my mind clicked back to an embarrassing situation Monica had recounted during her first month of work.

There had been a meeting on HIV/AIDS in the Ministry of Health and Monica wanted to be on time, in fact she got there a bit in advance. As the meeting time got closer and no one else had arrived, she decided to go to another office to see if the meeting was cancelled. "Oh no, the meeting was held at two o'clock as scheduled," said the secretary. Turns out, Ethiopian time two o'clock was actually eight in the morning Western time!

In making appointments with Ethiopians, I had to clarify whether I was talking about *habesha* time or *ferenj* time. According to *habesha* (or Ethiopian) time, the day is split into two twelve-hour halves. The "day" half began at six in the morning and ended at six in the evening. The "night" half was from six in the evening until six in the morning. In Ethiopia, daylight and sunset occurred near the changes between these halves. So, seven in the morning in the East African time zone for Ethiopia is one o'clock in local Ethiopian time. If I wanted to leave at eight in the morning *ferenj* time, that translated to two o'clock in the morning in *habesha* time. Likewise, if I wanted to leave at the latest by four in the evening *ferenj* time, that translated into ten o'clock *habesha* time. Telling *habesha* time took some getting used to for me. I must confess I usually said, "I would like to leave at seven in the morning *ferenj* time!" and leave the driver to figure out *habesha* time. I never personally had a problem with time at work, because the UN system and Western organizations ran on *ferenj* time. Difficulty arose when dealing with government-arranged meetings, Ethiopian festivities, or invitations for an event at an Ethiopian home. I would double-check with Ethiopian staff to make sure I knew when to arrive.

And I was off to Awasa, the capital city of Sidamo province, to meet the provincial health staff and to find out how they controlled meningitis outbreaks. We left early and headed south. Some five hours later, we arrived at our destination. The provincial authorities had received word I was coming, and they were ready to provide an overview and the charts of the patients. A total of three young adults and one child had been seen over a three-week period. Only one case was still in the hospital. In reviewing the charts (and I use the word "reviewing" loosely, because some of the script was in Amharic), I noticed the dates were written in the Arabic numeral system with (EC) following them: Tikemet 1983 EC (Ethiopian Calendar). However, the date as far as I was concerned was *October 1990*. I was expecting this date discrepancy, as Monica had recounted another problem she had early on in her assignment.

When Monica first visited the Ministry of Health's HIV warehouse in 1988, she was horrified to see they were using HIV test kits that had clearly expired (expiration date: 1983). The warehouse staff could not understand why she was having a hissy fit, because they only spoke Amharic. She headed back to the office all distraught, until an Ethiopian technical staff member came by who explained that the forms were filled out according to the Ethiopian calendar. So 1983 EC was actually Western calendar 1990. After Monica calmed down, she had a series of date calendar stamps made up in Western calendar dates and both dates were to be placed on forms.

So why does the Ethiopian calendar differ from the Western, or Gregorian, calendar? Historical literature established that the calendars of the entire world were based on the work of the old Egyptian astronomers who discovered, as early as 3000 BC to 4000 BC that the solar year lasted slightly less than 365 ¼ days. However, it was left to the astronomers of the Alexandrian

(Coptic) school to incorporate this knowledge into some sort of calendar; it was these astronomers who also came up with the idea of leap years.

The Gregorian calendar is the most widely used calendar in the world. Its predecessor, the Julian calendar, was replaced because the formula it used to calculate leap years produced a leap year every four years, which (apparently) was too many. The Gregorian calendar used a more accurate rule for calculating leap years.

The Ethiopian calendar, also called the *Ge'ez* calendar, is the principal calendar used in Ethiopia, and also serves as the liturgical calendar for Christians in Ethiopia and Eritrea belonging to the Orthodox Tewahedo Church, Eastern Catholic Churches, and Coptic Orthodox Church of Alexandria. It is based on the older Coptic calendar, which adds a leap day every four years without exception and begins the year on August 29 or August 30. A seven-to-eight-year gap between the Ethiopian and Gregorian calendars results from differing calculations in determining the date of the Annunciation of Jesus (i.e., the date when the Angel Gabriel announced to the Virgin Mary that she would conceive the Christ child).

The Ethiopian Orthodox church did not agree to the new calculations for the date—which was, however, eventually adopted by most other churches around the world. It took around three hundred years for most churches to agree. *The Ethiopian Orthodox calendar is now seven or eight years behind Western calendars.* Since this dichotomy existed between the two calendars, I liked to think that in Ethiopia I was seven years younger!

Like the Coptic calendar, the Ethiopian calendar has twelve months of thirty days each, plus five or six *epagomenal* (leap days to make the calendar follow the moon phases). In Ethiopia, this comprised a thirteenth month. I spent considerable time trying, for example, to calculate how old a child was or the date an infection started to get worse. Even with a nurse interpreter talking to the mother, trying to determine dates was difficult. I needed to identify important local events that had a known Ethiopian date, and then extrapolate to the Western calendar. A mother would know, for example, that her child was born the year of the big drought, or the year Haile Selassie died. In the end, for future field trips, I eventually made up my own handy calendar to help me figure out the dates of the year according to the Western calendar. That said, Ethiopia developed this catchy tourism phrase—*thirteen months of sunshine*. And one would see this phrase on posters and tourist brochures for the country.

In going to Sidamo province, I knew I would see how the Provincial Health Office handled sporadic, endemic cases of meningitis. I would be able to evaluate their knowledge of meningitis and get an idea of resources at both the provincial and district level and what supplies and medicines were readily available. The one patient still in the hospital was a six-year-old male child. He had arrived six days previously, presenting with fever, vomiting, and a stiff neck—classic signs and symptoms of meningitis. No one else was sick at home in his family.

I knew that transmission of *N. meningitidis* occurs from person to person, usually from a carrier rather than from a person who has meningitis, through contact with respiratory droplets or oral secretions. The "carrier" usually has no symptoms and is not ill! And from the history of this little boy, no other person was ill at home. Contagiousness rapidly disappears in patients once they start on antibiotic therapy. Since the meningococcus is relatively susceptible to temperature changes and dryness, the organism is not transmitted through shared equipment or other materials. So neither isolation of the patient nor disinfection of the room was necessary. This patient, in fact, was on the pediatric ward.

The six-year-old patient had a lumbar puncture and the provincial laboratory determined it was positive. He was started on IV treatment immediately. The three other young adult cases came from different geographic locations in the province over a three-week period. And there had been no further cases identified for more than a week.

Risk factors for invasive disease and for outbreaks are not completely understood. But in taking the history from the mother, we knew the child had not traveled outside his village. And no climatic factors came into play such as dust storms or drought. So clearly we were dealing with a sporadic case.

In most developing countries, health facilities lack supplies, drugs, and laboratory equipment. Because I was at a provincial hospital, it had more supplies and staff than what was available at a district or health center level. Intravenous chloramphenicol was available. However, if one was dealing with an outbreak where the ward had 100 cases, nurses would not be able to keep IVs going in that many cases with limited staff. In the case of an outbreak, the majority of patients can be treated with a single dose of long-acting oily chloramphenicol if available.

If Ethiopia had another epidemic, we would also need the A/C meningococcal vaccines, which were extremely effective. When used in rapid mass campaigns, vaccination could contain an outbreak within two to three weeks.

In the end, the field trip was important because I could see what medications were available at the provincial level. Medications for common ailments were available, and the antibiotic to treat meningitis was plentiful. However, oily chloramphenicol was not available, and neither were meningitis vaccines. The province communicated with the capital, Addis Ababa, by radio in emergencies, to alert them and also to obtain needed supplies. The information I gathered would come in handy in developing the guidelines. Would we be able to get everything in place before an actual outbreak occurred? Only time would tell. The first step was developing a plan, but it was not clear to me from where the resources would come for the vaccines and medications. And then we also needed to train all the health staff and pre-position supplies.

The following morning, as my vehicle headed back to the capital, I had ample time to reflect on all the things required for a rapid response to a meningitis epidemic. And then I suddenly realized I'd been in Ethiopia for five weeks already, yet I had not touched base with the Ministry of Labour and Social Welfare to see Werkesentayhu to find out exactly what documents were needed in the adoption packet.

Chapter 6

Disease Committee

As soon as I got back from Sidamo province, I paid a visit to Werkesentayhu.

"Surprise!" I said. "I accepted the job and now I'm living in Addis. What documents do I need to submit to you?"

And so he outlined the legal papers to be submitted in one adoption packet. The following were mandatory: a medical certificate stating I was healthy, an original birth certificate, financial proof of being capable of supporting a child, a home study conducted by a social worker, three references by people who knew me well and could vouch as to my fitness to raise a child, a letter of good moral conduct issued by the police department from the state where I resided in the US before arriving in Ethiopia, fingerprints, and two passport-size photos.

"Dr. Davis," Werke said, "remember that the adoption packet must be complete before submission to the committee, and any references you receive in English must be translated into Amharic."

"How long does the process take from submission to approval?"

Werke smiled and said, "That depends on how many people are in line ahead of you. Adoption packets are examined in order of arrival. There are three members on the committee, and everyone has to read the documents and make an independent decision before meeting as a group to discuss the case. We meet once a week. It's best to get your documents submitted as soon as possible!"

And he went back to reading a stack of documents on his desk.

I headed back to the WHO/EPR Centre located in the UN's Economic Commission for Africa (ECA) building. I had a lot to think about. The documents they wanted were not so onerous to obtain, except for that letter of good moral conduct from the police. Which friends should I ask to write a reference? They probably should be married with kids. And how was I supposed to get this letter of good moral conduct? I'd basically been out of the US since 1981. The police in my hometown of Walnut Creek, California had no idea what I had been doing since I left medical school. And I needed to find a social worker to conduct the home study. Right, Connie! I needed a home study and I didn't even have housing. I needed to go by WHO/Administration and explain why I requested a house and not an apartment to live in. And I'd best get off letters to friends asking for their references. Maybe I could ask Monica if she would be a reference?

Soon after my return from Sidamo, I was pleasantly surprised to have an official letter from the Ministry stating who was nominated for the meningitis guidelines development committee. We would be a total of five and I was nominated the president of the committee. Since I was president I could convoke the meetings, so I sent off invitations immediately. I noted that one member was an infectious disease specialist, while another had formulated health emergency guidelines on cholera. Another was a district health officer from Addis. Their diversity would be helpful because they could ask the bureaucracy for guidelines that were already formulated and might need some tweaking. And the officer who worked at the district level would know how communication and supervision was currently done between provinces to the federal level, and how supplies were ordered. And more importantly, who paid for supplies and medicines. The WHO country office probably had reports on disease outbreaks and the last epidemic of meningitis in Ethiopia.

The first orientation meeting was informative. I presented an overview of the task of the committee and the urgency to develop practical guidelines that would provide concise instructions for the identification of a meningitis outbreak. It had to include the steps necessary to confirm it, the required lab exams, appropriate treatment, and the necessity for stockpiling vaccines and medicines. We would need to develop a simplified way to rapidly report cases to the capital by radio. Time would be of the essence. Some districts might need additional emergency personnel to help handle the outbreak.

It became apparent that while this task might be my primary project, the other members had their regular work to do in hospitals or clinics. We discussed their availability to work on the committee and how we might set it up to be most efficient. For starters, I needed documents that spelled out the functioning of the different health staff at the *kebele*, district, and provincial levels and how emergencies were currently handled. And then we could discuss how meningitis should be handled to reduce morbidity and mortality. We made a list of the key documents to obtain, and who would collect them. I would be in charge of setting up reference files for the documents, scheduling meeting rooms, and assigning writing tasks. English was the second or third language for most, so it was clear I would be the main writer of the guidelines. I would get "drafts" on certain subjects from the members, but they looked to me for the organization of the template guidelines and editing. I would draft most sections and distribute the drafts before meetings, so the members could review and make comments for revision.

The days were getting colder. By November 1990 (in the Gregorian calendar), the committee had collected the majority of the official documents. Since Ethiopia was new to me, I had a lot of reading to do to understand how the health system worked. But in general, I thought the committee was making progress and soon we could start discussions on what had been the constraints in previous outbreaks and what new ideas would be needed to rapidly control outbreaks in the Ethiopian context. Then I got an email from AFRO. Both Chad and Sudan were reporting meningitis outbreaks and were requesting technical assistance from the regional program in Brazzaville. AFRO was requesting that I provide that assistance. Neither country was in my sphere of operation; I was supposed to provide assistance to Ethiopia and Uganda. So I got on the phone to Brazzaville to see what they wanted.

AFRO wanted me to go to Chad, as they could easily obtain country clearance for me. For some reason, Sudan was not expediting a visa. I checked with my director and he advised I could use the funds that supported me to go to Chad even though it was outside my assigned territory. What was the point of having an assigned project territory if I could be pulled to respond to all outbreaks? On the one hand, I would not meet my goals of getting the manuals developed for Ethiopia. I would be evaluated on that task. On the other hand, I had a real epidemic to confront in Chad, and getting experience in an epidemic was worth more than any book learning. When I returned, I could speak to my director about how to field continuing requests versus completing my project tasks.

Chapter 7

Outbreak

I left for the Ghion Hotel to start packing for Chad. The Republic of Chad was a landlocked country in Central Africa. It was bordered by Libya to the north, Sudan to the east, the Central African Republic to the south, Cameroon and Nigeria to the southwest, and Niger to the west. I knew relatively little about Chad except that at one point it was a French colony. I think it was fair to say that in the French scale of priorities, the colony of Chad ranked close to the bottom. It was looked on primarily as a source of raw cotton and untrained labor to be used in the more productive francophone colonies to the south. At the time I went in 1990, it had little political stability and widespread poverty. Not too many tourists made their way to Chad. Ethiopian Airlines did have one flight a week from Addis, which I was to leave on the next day. It would be tight for me to get travel documents and per diem for the trip. The admin office would not be pleased. Usually I needed to give several days for them to organize money.

It was an early morning flight, and I was at Bole Airport waiting for the call to board. The flight would take about five hours. In those days, Ethiopian Airlines had a policy that all passengers had to identify their luggage before they got on the plane. I was one of the first at the gate and off to locate my luggage. It was lined up on the tarmac to be identified for the ground crew to transfer to the carts bound for the plane. It was only one bag, but I couldn't find it. I systematically went down one row on the tarmac, and up another. I couldn't find my bag! Others had located theirs, and only three bags remained on the asphalt. I told one of the ground crew that my bag was missing, and he said, "No, it's already on the plane." Oh really! It didn't sound right, but I didn't want to make a scene, so I reluctantly started up the stairs of the plane.

I was the last one to board, so I moved quickly to find my seat. The regional WHO office told me that the WHO car would meet me at the airport. As I settled down in my seat, I dozed off for the five-hour flight and didn't wake until the pilot announced our imminent landing. As I walked off the plane, I was hit by a furnace blast of heat. The WHO driver was there with a sign with my name and he showed me the way to the luggage carousel. Only problem—my suitcase wasn't there. When they finally stopped the conveyor, I reluctantly came to terms that I was screwed. I couldn't believe this was happening to me! The flight was only once a week, so I would have to make do with what I was wearing. I was not happy over in Lost and Found.

As I planned to leave in one week, I told them, "Do not put my luggage on the returning flight! Just hold it in Bole Airport!" The officer gave me the equivalent of twenty USD as lost luggage compensation and waved me on my way. Welcome to Chad!

I looked at the driver and said, "Take me to the hotel and let me check in so at least I'll have a room somewhere."

Now I always carried an extra set of underwear and a T-shirt top with me in my hand luggage, but I did not look forward to washing laundry every night. With the room assured, we headed to the WHO country office.

The representative was sorry about the missing luggage. "The driver who picked you up at the airport will be with you all the time in N'Djamena," he said. "He can take you to the Grande Marche sometime today to look for clothes, though I doubt you will find anything to your liking. The Ministry of Health is anxiously awaiting your arrival and the driver knows where everyone is located. Let me know if you need any other assistance."

And I was off to find the doctor in charge of handling the emergency. It was now late afternoon, but the Head of Communicable Diseases was still in his office.

He looked up from his desk and smiled and said, "Welcome to N'Djamena, Dr. Davis, and glad you could assist us!" He then launched into a brief summary of when the meningitis outbreak started, which was ten days ago. They had admitted 123 people to the main hospital to date, and it showed no signs of lessening. Yes, we had an epidemic on our hands. Initially, they thought the infection had started in the outskirts of the capital. It was only later that they learned the first person admitted was not from the capital but had come in from another district to visit his family members in town and then had taken sick. They were getting ill people from outside the capital and were trying to call the outlying districts to find out their situation. Key people met at his office every morning to provide updates as to new cases.

"Have you started a line listing of patients as they came into the hospital, along with their symptoms, date for the start of illness and their village name?" I asked. To determine whether you have an epidemic, you need to know when the first case was, if the cases are coming from one village or district or several, and if cases are doubling in one week. With the use of a map, one can identify where you should target your resources.

"We started two days ago, but the line listing is not yet complete. We hope to have it done by tomorrow morning."

"I want to drop by the hospital now, to get an overview of the situation, but will return tomorrow to go in depth into the laboratory results and history of the patients."

And we took off for the hospital. We met the Chief Medical Officer and visited the wards—two large rooms segregated by gender. The wards had forty beds in each room. They had run out of beds, so about twenty patients were lying on straw mats on the concrete floor in each ward. The pediatric ward also had about eight patients. The wards were congested because in Africa the patient has to be accompanied by a family member who can provide meals for them. N'Djamena is hot and humid. Overhead fans whirred, but the air hung oppressively over the wards. All available staff, both nurses and doctors, were called in to be put on special schedules to handle the cases.

We needed to determine where most of these cases were from, so we could try and treat patients closer to their homes and relieve the pressure on the main hospital. But people come to the main hospital because they know it probably has more medicines and supplies. I was taking notes, but I thought the Ministry of Health needed to issue a public service announcement (PSA) on the radio soon and give explicit directions to sick people to go to their nearest health center. They did have supplies and medicines. And unless people were seriously ill, they needed to stay home because staff were focused on the epidemic.

It was already dark when I left the hospital, but there was still time to swing by the market to buy some type of shirt. The traditional clothing for women in Chad was two types of *pagnes* (rectangular pieces of cloth about four feet long), wrapped around the body. I found something called a *boubou* that hit at just above the ankles and could be worn as a type of caftan. I could switch between it and my cotton pants. Not convenient, but it worked.

I was glad to return to the hotel since I had started the day at five in the morning in Addis. In emergency situations it is easy to get overwhelmed and to continue to push yourself. So it's important to eat and to get sleep if you want to continue to be effective. I needed a warm shower to relax my muscles. The hotel had air conditioning, so the windows could stay shut from the mosquitoes that transmit malaria. I washed my underwear and worked on the PSA before I fell off into a deep sleep.

The next morning at the daily emergency meeting, we found out patients were continuing to be admitted. This gave impetus to completing the line listing of patients and identifying the affected districts. I gave the emergency team the draft PSA I had worked on the night before. The country had a previous epidemic in 1988 and they were using IV chloramphenicol, but changing IVs and giving medications on time over seven days was overwhelming the nurses. If we could find the locus of the infection, we could better target and contain the spread by doing preventive vaccinations. I returned to the WHO office to send out an urgent request to both AFRO and Geneva to request assistance in obtaining vaccines and oily chloramphenicol. Finally, an updated line listing of cases identified the probable contiguous district. I made plans to visit that district hospital with other government officials the next day. The Ministry of Health issued a clear PSA on the outbreak that evening to address community concerns and to ask those who were sick to immediately seek care at the closest health facility.

We left for the concerned district in the early afternoon and were soon at the hospital to assess their handling of cases. Obviously poor communication (the telephone line was down), lack of adequate logistics (the district had only one working vehicle), and limited staff made treating cases a nightmare. Our team brought two nurses to help in treatment of cases at the district hospital. The team also carried supplemental antibiotics and vaccines left over from the 1988 outbreak. Working with the district medical officer, we identified the area where preventive vaccination could have the most effect. We went out to the affected villages and told the village headmen that vaccination would start tomorrow. Clearly, having guidelines in place and pre-positioned drugs and vaccines in selected areas could have rapidly stopped this outbreak. It showed the importance and the need for the WHO/EPR Centre to develop the guidelines quickly and to provide the technical expertise and training to countries to implement them. But all of this would require funding and additional staff.

On return to the capital in the evening, I had a message on my desk from the Chad WHO Country Representative. Geneva had located meningococcal vaccines and oily chloramphenicol and was expediting their delivery the next day. I was thankful Geneva had some supplies on hand, but I worried about how one would get funding to implement this program region wide. It's all well and good to develop country plans, but it would take solid funding to implement these plans. That was for another day; right now we needed to halt this outbreak.

I continued working with the emergency unit in updating the line listing, which now showed a decrease in daily cases. The Geneva supplies arrived the next day and were quickly expedited through customs and distributed rapidly to the concerned districts. Once the outlying districts implemented preventive vaccinations, new cases started to dramatically decrease. We also saw a decrease in the numbers of cases coming to the hospital in the capital. The use of one injection of oily chloramphenicol dramatically lessened the work of the nurses on the wards. Some treated patients started to go home. The emergency team could finally see the result of their efforts. We all breathed a collective sigh of relief. We were winning this battle. I could head home to Ethiopia knowing the outbreak was under control. But I worried that my next outbreak would be in Ethiopia, and we were not prepared.

Chapter 8

Festivities

I was looking forward to the Christmas holidays. In the rush to respond to the Chad meningitis outbreak, Thanksgiving had somehow slipped my mind. So I was somewhat taken aback that Ethiopians wouldn't celebrate on December 25, but Christmas (or *Genna*) was celebrated according to the Orthodox Church on January 7. Prior to Ethiopia, I had worked in a Muslim majority country—Senegal—and Christmas celebrations were rather pathetic affairs confined to five-star hotels with plastic Christmas trees and sweat profusely running down your face while standing around a fake fireplace. But Addis was a UN hub and Ethiopia was a Christian country, and numerous regional organizations were based in Addis. The holiday season proved to be considerably livelier. The numerous nongovernmental organizations (NGOs) used this occasion to sell handcrafted articles that their constituency made. Plenty of Christmas markets were set up in major hotels or in the compounds of larger NGOs with special stalls, and one could find exquisite gold and silver jewelry, handmade shawls, Ethiopian artwork, books, tableware, candles, and incense. Whatever you could dream, they had made it. This was the time to pick up one-of-a-kind gifts for when you eventually got to go on home leave.

I especially liked the exhibitions at the Hilton, which provided space in a huge conference hall decorated in bright Christmas colors and real Christmas trees. Seasonal music played over the loud speakers and the scent of cinnamon and cardamom drifted in the air. Monica and I would wander down the lanes where items were beautifully presented in a tempting array. I picked up little gifts of candles, incense, and hand-painted writing paper to give away at the numerous parties where I was invited. For close friends I got exquisite woven shawls—not only beautiful but also necessary in the winter in Addis. I chose a beautiful embroidered tablecloth and napkins for my mom. And when our feet started to hurt and our tummies growled, we would wander over to one of the many restaurants to get recharged.

Between the parties celebrated at the office and those on the weekends, it was quite festive for those of us not traveling home during the holidays. And the great thing about Ethiopia was that I got to celebrate twice! However, Ethiopian *Genna* would be more of a spiritual and religious occasion, as they had no custom of exchanging gifts. It was a time to visit and focus on family members and to prepare special foods, relax, and play games.

Yet I detected unease. As one drove farther away from the central area around the ECA building and diplomatic holdings, the street lighting was subdued. The normal hustle and bustle was diminished. It took me a while to discern the difference. Significantly fewer people were in the street, and they all walked resolutely, with their heads down and rushing as if to escape a sudden hurricane warning. Their white *shammas* (cotton shawls) were pulled tightly around the head and shoulders, partially hiding the face. Now it struck me! No young boys or men were in the streets where usually, at dusk, the only people out in the streets were men. It was hard to know the daily news if you didn't have a shortwave radio. No English newspaper existed, and TV was only available in the lobby at the Ghion. The DERG was mute about the progress of the war.

I routinely headed for work early in order to avoid traffic and to concentrate on the documents and jot down notes before the phones started ringing. One morning in mid-December, I noticed an ominous bus, creeping along with all the windows covered with dark cloth as if it were going to a funeral service. When I arrived at the office, the director's secretary was already at her desk typing. I stopped at her desk.

"Maryam, can I ask you something? Today, I passed this bus on my way to the ECA. All the windows were covered in dark material. It felt sinister!"

She furtively looked around the office and motioned for me to sit down. "Young people—men and boys as young as fourteen—are disappearing from Addis! They say they're being sent up north to fight in the war. So people are hiding their family members from the military government. We don't get much news from the government, but it seems the war is going badly."

I was eager to ask more questions, but Maryam clearly didn't want to talk about the situation. I suppose the less said, the better for all concerned. I went to my office and pulled out sections of the emergency preparedness manual. Yet my heart wasn't into working on the document. I needed to find out more about the war in the North, but how?

Chapter 9

Addis Routine

Back in my office at the WHO/EPR Centre, I wrote up my trip report for Chad and followed up on the arrival of all the supplies requested by the Chad Ministry of Health. And I needed to find out if any of the guidelines team would be available over the December holidays to work on the Ethiopian meningitis guidelines. Then the phone rang, and Monica informed me about a "new" restaurant. She thought we needed a dinner out. In those days, few restaurants offered something different from Ethiopian cuisine. For important occasions, Castelli's Italian restaurant was a longtime favorite that required reservations. Castelli's grew their own veggies, made their pastas by hand, and imported great Italian wines. It was considered expensive, but it was worth it for special occasions. But Monica was gushing with praise for the Armenian Club.

"Connie, this yogurt soup is to die for!" she said when we met. "But you must become a member to eat there. I have the form for you to fill out."

"Monica, I'm not Armenian, and unless I'm mistaken, you're not either!"

She smiled and pulled out her membership card. "I do have distant relatives," she said with a smile. "And I can invite close friends to join."

That's how I became a member of the Armenian Club. It was located centrally and easy to slip in for a quick lunch of *kibbeh* (cucumber/yogurt soup) and lamb kabobs.

Monica also introduced me early on to her favorite haunts up in the Piazza in Old Town and along Churchill Road. Usually on a Sunday after meeting friends for brunch at the Hilton, Monica and I would head out on a shopping expedition looking for antique Ethiopian silver jewelry. I first began collecting antique silver jewelry in my India days. Silver was less expensive than gold, and it was striking on my skin tone. I wasn't in Ethiopia long before I noticed the silver and brass neck crosses that adorned both male and female Coptic Christians. In the fifteenth century, the Emperor Zara Yaqob decreed that all Christians should wear a neck cross so they could be easily distinguished from non-believers. Yaqob was, at the time, fighting Muslim invaders in the kingdom.

I wanted to collect silver crosses representing each of the cities, towns, and regions of Ethiopia. One antique shop up in the Piazza had a great selection of crosses. We called the shopkeepers "The Sharks" because they were skilled at identifying exactly what you wanted. They also knew the price each of us was willing to cough up to obtain a select silver item. The shop was rather nondescript on the outside. Windows framed either side of the narrow doorway, and peering into the shop revealed an eclectic jumble of Ethiopian swords, old rifles from the nineteenth century, handmade baby carriers with cowrie shells outlining the leather perimeter, and old photographs of Haile Selassie and previous emperors. But no silver crosses graced the window display.

Once inside the shop, only one small display case contained crosses from Lalibela and Addis Ababa. The owner waited for you to ask about silver crosses and, if he thought you might be a connoisseur, he invited you into the inner sanctum. The hideaway was not very large, but necklaces, bracelets, and crosses covered every inch of the walls. Since Monica and I became loyal customers, he would reach under a table and haul out a six-gallon cotton hemp sack and slam it on the coffee table. With one deft movement of the hand, he upturned the sack and out spilled 250 old silver crosses of varying sizes. The first time he did that, I just stared mesmerized by the quantity and quality of the crosses. And he left us in the room to pull out crosses that interested us or throw them back on the pile.

Thirty minutes later, he would return to answer our questions. "Yes, this one is from Gonder, and this is from Welega. Now look at this one—they just cut a cross shape out of the Maria Theresa thaler. You don't see too many of those," he said. And he pulled out his old coin collection and showed us the thaler. The Maria Theresa thaler was a silver bullion coin used continuously in world trade since it was first minted in 1741 in Austria. The silver thaler became a trade coin not only in Ethiopia, but was also used even more widely throughout much of Arabia and the Horn of Africa.

Ancient crosses were initially made of brass and wood, particularly the large processional crosses carried by the priests. These processional crosses were made by the *lost wax technique* in metal workshops located in close proximity to the monasteries of the Orthodox Church.

The lost wax process was time consuming and began with beeswax, or another material with a low melting point. It must be soft enough for carving fine details, but hard enough to retain its shape. After the wax object has been carved, increasingly coarse layers of clay are applied to the object and allowed to dry. The first and finest clay slips capture the wax details in the smooth mold, and the coarser clay layers provide strength. Holes are left at both ends of the clay mold. The entire assemblage is fired, causing the original wax carving to melt and drain away, leaving only a baked clay shell. Liquid metal is then poured into the empty mold and left to cool and harden. Later, the clay exterior is broken open, revealing the finished metal object beneath. In direct lost wax casting, the object produced is always unique, as the clay mold is necessarily destroyed as part of the casting process.

In Ethiopia, I repeatedly tried to see the entire process from beginning to end, but I only managed to arrive at the end stages to see them finishing the metal.

I was always on the search for new and unusual cross designs, and by the time I left Ethiopia I had quite a collection.

Chapter 10

Fingerprints

The Western Christmas festivities were over, but now it was January 1991 and Ethiopian Christmas was fast approaching. I gave myself until the end of January to collect all the documents that needed to be in the adoption dossier. My references came through with flying colors. Both my Belgian friends in Senegal and my UK friends working in Poland had promptly written and sent their reference letters to me. And I don't know how they did it, but they both had gotten the documents translated into Amharic! Monica told me her letter was written, but it was still being translated. I already had most of the documents like the original copy of my birth certificate. I also had financial documents to prove I could support a child. But I needed to get a home study conducted by a social worker. And how would I obtain this certificate of good moral character. I decided I had best go to the US Embassy and see the Consular Section. They would certainly know about intercountry adoptions and what was necessary as far as the American government was concerned.

I got an appointment right away and went in to see the consular officer. He wanted to know if I planned to adopt in-country or adopt in the US.

"I'll adopt in Ethiopia," I said. "I'll be working for WHO for at least two years, and I thought the process would be easier and more economical in Ethiopia."

"That sounds like a good plan, but make sure the home study is done by a social worker who is licensed in Ethiopia but also has international credentials acceptable to the US." And then he said, "At the embassy, we also have a list of physicians approved to do the child's physical, so be sure and contact us when you're at that stage of the process. But the most important thing is that the child must be free of HIV/AIDS to enter the US. So he or she should be tested at the first possible opportunity, before you become attached to the child." Great! Monica would know where I could get the HIV testing done.

He suggested I call some NGOs that worked in health. They would have on staff, or know of, appropriate social workers who could help me. However, it was Monica who found me an American social worker working for an NGO who was certified to do home studies. Now comes the hard part, I thought.

As I left the US Embassy, I noticed the light was fading rapidly. January in Addis Ababa generally had sunny days, but when the sun started to set the temperature could drop quite fast at eight thousand feet altitude. I pulled my woolen sweater around me as I made my way to the car. I was looking forward to my room in the Ghion and getting a fire roaring in the fireplace. This seemed to be a good time to order up pasta and beer to the room. Soon a crackling fire was blazing in the fireplace and I could remove my sweater and just gaze into the hearth. This whole adoption process was challenging, intrusive, and time consuming, and it wasn't clear how expensive adopting would be in Ethiopia! Certainly in the States, adoption was pricey! What's more, I'd need to convince a total stranger I was fit and capable of being a parent. It didn't seem fair that the adoptive parent had to negotiate this emotional minefield and yet the biological parent never had to go through this invasive scrutiny. Did I really want to go through with this? It would actually be easier for me to find some attractive guy and have sex and then just never tell him I was pregnant and simply disappear. But that went against all my religious beliefs and sense of integrity. And why bring another child into the world when plenty of children needed adoptive parents? So I had to come up with answers for this home study interview. I was fairly certain as to the first question. "Why do you want to adopt?"

    I don't remember ever having dreams about getting married and having a big house and two children. My dreams had always been about being a doctor. I hadn't been sure what type of doctor—whether a surgeon like my dad, or a pediatrician. It just was a given. And somewhere along the way I would meet this handsome guy and we would fall in love and get married. I didn't fantasize about marriage; I worried about getting into medical school. And after that, I figured the rest would fall into place. I met scores of guys along the way. Some had no intention of ever settling down and marrying. Others wanted to get married someday, just not then. And if truth be told, I also wanted to see new places, explore lost worlds, and travel to exotic locations. I came close several times to thinking, this was the man! But in the end, I chickened out. And now close to being forty-four years old, it was a little late trying to track down former lovers to see where they were. They say you can't go back again. And then one day you realize that one part of your life had turned out the way you wanted, but the other had not.

    Why did I want to adopt? I wanted a family. I wanted an infant to raise and see the child go through all the "milestones."

However, when I had investigated domestic adoption in Atlanta some ten years earlier, they had been pretty dismissive of "older" mothers. The adoption agencies I had talked to had been quite blunt in that an older, single woman would never get an infant. Infants were in short supply. If a single woman wanted to adopt, she should be ready to take an older child *and* one with disabilities. But my work was in international public health and in getting assigned overseas to countries with poor or nonexistent health facilities. I needed, along with any family members, to be able to obtain a worldwide available (Class 1) clearance that attested to no identifiable medical conditions that would limit assignment abroad. Before each new posting, I went through a rigorous health exam. If I had a child with disabilities who needed specialized care, or specialized medications, I would be limited to domestic postings. I wasn't looking for a "gifted" child, but I did need a healthy one!

I had another deep desire for wanting to adopt an Ethiopian infant girl. A cultural practice occurred in certain African and Middle Eastern countries, including Ethiopia, called *female genital mutilation*. Sometimes called female genital cutting or female circumcision, it is the ritual cutting or removal of some or all of the external female genitalia. Typically carried out by a traditional woman circumciser using a non-sterile blade, female genital mutilation (FGM) is conducted at eight days after birth, at puberty, or sometimes right before marriage.

The practice is rooted in gender inequality, attempts to control women's sexuality, and ideas about purity, modesty, and beauty. It is usually initiated and carried out by women, who see it as a source of honor, and who fear that failing to have their daughters and granddaughters cut will expose the girls to ostracism. Significant side effects depend on the severity of the procedure. Those who undergo "the cut" can suffer recurrent bladder infections, difficulty urinating and passing menstrual flow, chronic pain, the development of cysts, an inability to get pregnant, complications during childbirth, and fatal bleeding. *There are no known health benefits* for this cultural practice. I wanted a baby girl and I wanted to locate her before she went through a traumatizing event.

I had initially come across this practice when I was doing a nutritional survey in Somalia in 1980. At first I thought it was associated only with Muslim communities even though this procedure is *not* a tenet of the religion. As I dug deeper into Ethiopian culture, I discovered that female genital mutilation crossed all ethnic and religious communities. It seemed to me that the younger the child, the less likely she would have undergone this procedure. Consequently, I wanted to adopt a young infant. But I didn't think sharing this motivation would be particularly helpful in the home study interview.

As far as being a good parent, I thought I could be a great mom. I looked and felt young, and I still had enough energy to take care of a baby. I could introduce her to the things I was passionate about: horseback riding, tennis, hiking in the mountains, and travel. When the child was ten, I would only be 55 years old. When she was 18, I would be 63, and she would be heading for college and having her own life. I did worry about being a single parent and the financial burden single parenthood entailed. If I stayed overseas and worked with international organizations, I could maintain the lifestyle to which I was accustomed and could afford whatever domestic house staff I might need, such as a housekeeper and ayah or nanny. If I continued my carefree single lifestyle, I would just spend more and more money on fabulous trips and ski vacations. I wanted to experience the world again through a child's eyes and relive holiday traditions like decorating the tree for Christmas, dying Easter eggs, picking out a costume for Halloween, and midnight Mass at Christmas. I got up and looked in my purse for the scrap of paper Monica had given me with the name of the social worker—Sara L. Right. I would call her the next day!

But I still needed fingerprints and this certificate of good moral character. Now, if I was still in the US I would go to the nearest police station. I guessed since I was a foreigner I should go to Interpol. I noticed they had an office in Addis. So at lunch I headed over to the office and asked the receptionist if I could talk to an officer.

I introduced myself and explained that I was adopting locally in Ethiopia and I needed a set of fingerprints. Could they do them for me?

The guy looked at me like I was crazy! "Dr. Davis, Interpol is involved in battling terrorism, crimes against humanity, genocide, and the like. We don't do fingerprints for the general public."

Muttering to myself, I said, "So where am I supposed to get these damn fingerprints done?"

And he looked at me and said, "You're American, right?"

I nodded, yes.

"Well, your embassy does fingerprints!"

Boy was I embarrassed, as I slunk out of the office. While I was getting an appointment to go back to the US Embassy, I decided to call Werkesentayhu. I explained that I had been working overseas for the UN for some ten years, so it was difficult to ask the police in the town where I grew up for this certificate of good morals, especially since I was not physically in the US. Werke suggested I go to the main police station in Addis and request a statement from them.

The last thing I wanted to do was to enter any Ethiopian police station. For starters we would probably have a language barrier, and then there would be dealing with the bureaucracy. So I called Monica that evening and nicely asked if she wanted to have a firsthand experience in visiting the police! I figured with Monica's almost white-blond hair and me looking Ethiopian, it would be a startling contrast that would get us fast attention and, hopefully, quick assistance. My intuition and foresight were right on. We got assistance immediately. It took a little explaining since my request for this certificate was not the usual request they got every day.

The officer wanted to be helpful and he said he could provide a statement that, since I had entered Ethiopia, the police had not received any reports of criminal activity performed by yours truly. He asked if I had any stationary with letterhead at my office?

"Sure, of course we do. But I need the stationary to say 'Ethiopian Police Station.'"

Then he explained that due to the war efforts, their budget was a little tight and they didn't have any stationary. If I brought the WHO stationary, they could type out the statement in Amharic and I would have what I needed.

Monica and I quickly ran out of the police station and looked at each and cracked up laughing. But it did make me wonder. How did they write up daily reports or criminal activities?

"I sure hope this works," I said shaking my head.

The next day, I delivered the stationary with letterhead and he told me when I could pick up the certificate. My home study interview was set for the end of the week. Once that was over, I would have all the documents I needed. What a relief to have all the official papers, I thought. One more national holiday was coming up in January—and on my birthday, January 19! The Ethiopian celebration of *Timket* (also known as Epiphany) was a symbolic reenactment of the baptism of Jesus in the River Jordan by John the Baptist. For Ethiopian Orthodox Christians, it served as a renewal of their baptismal vows.

Timket is a two-day festival, starting the day before, when the church *tabot* (replica of the Ark of the Covenant) is taken from the church to a nearby location, usually near a body of water. This is representative of Jesus going to the River Jordan. The *tabot* spends the night in this location while the priests and other faithful hold a vigil through the night. In the morning, the water is blessed and is then sprinkled on the gatherers (or they could choose to bathe in the water), renewing their baptismal vows. Long parades then carry the *tabot* back home to the church while the revelers sing and dance. The priests and acolytes are all decked out in rich colorful brocades, and the priests carry huge ornate processional crosses on staffs. A long line of celebrants follows the procession, singing and playing the drum or other musical instruments.

It was a photographers' paradise being able to freely take photos up close. I was surprised the priests let Monica and me approach so near. A rope barrier kept the faithful from getting too close, but the priests indicated to security to let us through. They were proud of their traditions and pleased we wanted to learn more. But it was also physically exhausting walking among the crush of celebrants, and we eventually peeled off and headed for the Wabi Shabelle Hotel to get something to eat.

The next day, I dropped by Monica's office in the national program on HIV/AIDS. She wanted to introduce me to someone who could eventually help me obtain an HIV/AIDS test for the infant when the time came. Dr. Debrework Zewdie, the deputy director and head of the Referral Laboratory for AIDS assured me that once I had found a child, she would come immediately to take the blood specimens and run the necessary tests. Since I was already out in the street, I drove back to the US Embassy. And yes, they did the fingerprints manually and gave me the prints in a sealed and stamped envelope.

Later that month, when the social worker arrived with the home study report she had prepared, I asked again, "You don't think it's a drawback not having a house or apartment to see to comment on the living space?"

"Not really," she responded. "The Ministry knows the situation in Addis that all foreigners have to wait for available lodging. Besides, all foreigners live in lodging comparable to landowners!"

And so, at last, I finally had all the required documents. I felt such relief that everything was finished, but the reality was I was just starting the process as far as the adoption committee was concerned. What I needed was patience, but what I thought was, Why wasn't there a "fast track" for candidates living and working in Ethiopia?

On the last day of January 1991, I headed once more to Werkesentayhu's office to deliver my dossier.

"So, how many people are ahead of me in the process?" I asked.

He smiled and rolled his eyes.

Chapter 11

Refugee Camp

It was now February 1991 and I was editing sections of the preparedness manual written by various members of the meningitis crisis group. The director of the WHO/EPR Centre called me to his office.

"Connie, the United Nations High Commissioner for Refugees has asked if we can send someone to investigate an illness in a Sudanese refugee camp located in the western part of Ethiopia. There have been a couple of deaths, and we're being asked to help out a sister agency."

"So, the UNHCR isn't suspecting anything to do with meningitis?" I queried.

He shook his head, no.

This was expected to be a quick turnaround investigation. So I packed my things and got ready to hop in a tiny six-seater airplane the next day, to travel to Gambela. They planned to drop me off, and a UN vehicle would take me to the camp. I would stay overnight, and then the plane would come back for me the next day. I liked little planes because of the different perspective of the earth as compared to flying in a huge jumbo jet. Those one-propeller planes didn't fly very high, maybe at ten thousand feet. So, flying over the savannah I could make out the individual *tukuls* (traditional thatched roof huts), with little wisps of smoke arising from the chimney, and the cattle or sheep in small herds. The plane seemed to float, peacefully and slowly like a bird in flight. As we approached the dirt runway, we made a sweep of the field to make sure no cattle were around and we made a quick direct approach. The UN vehicle was off to the side.

Two hours later, I was at the camp and meeting the staff. The camp was small, newly constructed in the middle of a semi-arid patch of land at the edge of a forest. It didn't have the typical UNHCR white tents but seemed to have "repurposed" wooden shed-like structures to hold the administrative unit, the medical dispensary, and a series of dormitories. The camp housed mostly young, single South Sudanese boys and men. So these were the *Lost Boys of Sudan,* I thought. This was the name given to a group of over 40,000 boys of the Nuer and Dinka ethnic groups. They had been displaced or orphaned during the Second Sudanese civil war (1987–2005). The boys had embarked on a treacherous land journey from Sudan to refugee camps in Ethiopia in search of food and security.

I met with the health staff, and they described a respiratory illness with coughing, fever but no rashes, and two deaths. We went on a quick tour of the premises. For starters, the camp dormitories were overcrowded—thirty to forty boys together in one long narrow room. The dormitories were wooden with an inadequate number of small windows that didn't provide enough ventilation for the heat and humidity inside the dorms. As I remember, the boys slept on cots spaced quite closely together. By cursory exam, they all appeared moderately to severely malnourished. Camp rations were minimal. There were outdoor latrines, but hygiene and sanitation could be improved. I can't remember what the water source was or whether it had to be trucked in. The rudimentary lab had not identified any bacterium in the cough samples collected. Whatever it was seemed to be viral. The boys had no school or other activities to engage them. They had to be bored.

I thought it best to try and segregate the sick together in one building to try to keep the healthy, healthy. Since the camp population was relatively young, they could be of help in improving the environment. It would also give them something to do. I suggested to the camp staff that they ask for volunteers and start a community health worker program to focus on getting clean water, identifying sick people to transport to the clinic, improving hygiene and sanitation, and making additional lodgings to reduce the overcrowding. The camp administration needed to request additional supplemental food and medicines urgently. I planned to carry back lab specimens the following day for additional tests in Addis. While there were probably good reasons to separate the young boys and men from the main camp of mostly women, it made for a strange environment. I made a separate report to UNHCR on the need for additional and better lodging and improved rations for the camp.

Chapter 12

US Staff Depart

Since I had submitted the adoption packet to the Ministry of Labour and Social Welfare, I started to get serious about looking for a teacher to learn Amharic. If I was going to adopt, then I should attempt to learn the language. At a minimum, I would need an Ethiopian ayah to help take care of the baby, and she would certainly not know English. So I started to look for a teacher in February 1991. I wanted to learn conversational Amharic but my eventual teacher, Berhanu, insisted that I needed to learn the Ethiopian script and alphabet first, because certain sounds could not be pronounced using only the Western English alphabet. I wasn't entirely convinced I needed to do that, but I didn't have a huge selection of teachers from which to choose. I was soon engrossed in trying to learn a complex series of letters, and the grammar was confusing—with verbs coming at the end of the sentence. Not to mention trying to reproduce the guttural sounds of the letters. It was rather daunting, and Amharic was certainly more difficult than when I learned French or Italian.

I was working in my office early March 1991, when I got a phone call from Monica.

"Connie, you're not going to believe this: the US Embassy has just authorized all nonessential staff to depart!"

"What do you mean? Why? I mean, the mood is ugly here in Addis, but I haven't heard the Ethiopian army has been losing any battles. In fact, I haven't recently seen those buses that used to pick up young boys and men conscripting them into the army."

"I need to contact my friends in the embassy and try to find out the low down," Monica said. "I doubt there will be much in the newspapers. But something must have happened!"

By evening, the town was abuzz with rampant rumors. Apparently, over the previous three weeks, the Ethiopian army had lost about one-fourth of the northern part of the country. The Tigrayan rebels had captured Gojam and Gonder! Gonder was an Ethiopian government stronghold in the North. How was this possible? And the Eritrean rebels were finally in control of the Red Sea port at Asab! This was astonishing, since the Ethiopian army was supposed to be so well-equipped by Russia with arms and military planes. If these rumors were true, then the country was landlocked without the port. Still, the prevailing sentiment among UN staff and NGOs was that the Americans were overreacting; there was no need to remove families and nonessential embassy staff at this point.

It was hard to have an informed opinion since low-level staff (myself included) were not in the loop of any UN meetings of consequence. But the word of the evacuation of American families certainly had a dampening effect on the morale of those left behind. I felt this unease, but I was too "new" to Addis to discern who truly knew what they were talking about. My intuition told me to look around, to ask questions, and to keep in close contact with the Ministry of Labour and Social Welfare (MLSW) and Werkesentayhu. I had progressed along the adoption system, and I felt that if the war escalated then it would be highly destabilizing. And it would be decidedly unlikely that I would be able to remain and work. I was stressed that if we were told to evacuate, then everything would stop as far as the adoption proceedings. This was not good news.

As I headed home to the Ghion, I thought back to my first visit to Ethiopia in the fall of 1989. I had visited the Lake Tana area and seen the thundering Blue Nile Falls and then had flown up to Gonder to visit the historical sights. Now Gonder was under rebel control! I got another call from Monica.

"Connie, come around to my apartment for a small get-together. I'm having some friends over to discuss whether we should be packing our bags!"

I jumped in the office loaner car to head to her place.

Only five of us went, all women, and most had already worked for about two years in Ethiopia. I didn't have much to say; but I had a whole lot to comprehend! One of the women—Joy—worked for UNHCR, had been in Addis for three years, and was something of a history buff.

"So tell me, Joy, why did the rebellion against the central government arise in the northern 'provinces' of Eritrea and Tigray," I said. "Ostensibly, both of these areas were part of the historic Ethiopian empire. Why did *they* want to secede?"

"Connie, to understand the problem you'll have to go back to the root of this whole trouble." "Does anyone remember in your history books something called the Scramble for Africa?" said Joy.

We all groaned, so she proceeded to enlighten us. Basically, it involved the invasion, occupation, division, colonization, and annexation of African territories by European powers during the late eighteenth century. Whenever you had European powers and riches to be made in Africa, there was bound to be some duplicity. Britain, Egypt, and Ethiopia signed a treaty at Adwa on June 3,

1884. The treaty provided that Ethiopia would have free transit for all goods, including arms, through the port of Massawa. And Britain was to protect and guarantee this right. Shortly after the treaty's ratification, the Italians occupied Massawa, the port previously held by Egypt. The British did nothing. This encouraged Italy to colonize Eritrea, and to deny Emperor Yohannes free and easy access to the port of Massawa. Without access to the port, Ethiopia was effectively a landlocked country!

The Italians wanted a colony and they started to penetrate Ethiopia up to the highlands, and Eritrea was formed in 1936 to 1941. But Italy was on the losing side in World War II.

"And we know what happens to losers," said Monica.

"Right," said Joy. "They lose their colonial possessions." Haile Selassie wanted Eritrea ceded to Ethiopia. The United Nations debated the fate of the former Italian colonies ad nauseam. The British and Americans preferred to cede Eritrea to the Ethiopians as a reward for their support during World War II. No one thought to ask the Eritrean people what they wanted.

"What happened?" I asked?

"So Eritrea was ceded to Ethiopia," said Joy. The UN General Assembly Resolution on December 2, 1950 called for Eritrea and Ethiopia to be linked through a loose federal structure under the sovereignty of the Emperor. Eritrea was to have its own administrative and judicial structure, its own flag, and control over its domestic affairs, including police, local administration, and taxation. The federal government (i.e., the existing imperial government) was to control foreign affairs (including commerce), defense, finance, and transportation.

"There was only one problem," said Joy. The bulk of Eritreans had developed a distinct sense of their own cultural identity and superiority vis-à-vis Ethiopians. They had a strong landowning peasantry and the virtual absence of serfdom. This, combined with the introduction of modern democracy during the few years that the British ruled in Eritrea, gave Eritreans a desire for political freedoms totally alien to traditional Ethiopian political ideas. This federation was doomed from the beginning, was my thought!

Haile Selassie did everything to undercut Eritrea's independent status. The Emperor pressured Eritrea's elected chief executive to resign, made Amharic the official language in place of Arabic and Tigrinya, terminated the use of the Eritrean flag, imposed censorship, and moved many businesses out of Eritrea. Clearly, this did little to inspire a sense of loyalty and love. Finally, in 1962 Haile Selassie pressured the Eritrean Assembly to abolish the Federation and join the Imperial Ethiopian fold. And so Eritrea became a "province" of Ethiopia. And therein was the start of their *War for Independence*.

"OK, I'm understanding Eritrea's discontent with Ethiopia, but Tigray has always been a province of Ethiopia. What's their beef?" I said.

"I've heard," said Monica, "that the Amhara people have always looked down on and marginalized the people from Tigray."

"It's complicated," said Joy. The discontent of Tigray province has always been stated as due to the deliberate marginalization of the Tigrayan people by the Amhara people (specifically the government in Addis Ababa).

"Yet," said Joy, "if you delve deeper into the issue and do some subsequent reading about the people of Tigray, it seems the peasants of Tigray were neither more nor less marginalized than Amharic-speaking peasants who lived in Gojam, Gonder, or Shewa."

The *senior elite* in Tigray was closely integrated with the imperial family through either marriage or business. It was a different story for those who would be considered *intermediate elites*. Those Tigrayans considered to rank in the intermediate level of society, and who would normally be considered for national administrative posts in Tigray and in other areas of Ethiopia, were the ones marginalized. These intermediate elites lost influence, initially over the highlands in Eritrea due to the colonizing effort done by Italy. And moreover, national administrative posts in Ethiopia went to elites from Shewa (the regional province from where Haile Selassie hailed).

After the "federation" of Eritrea to Ethiopia, the few government posts available for those outside of Shewa went to the Eritreans. So the Tigrayans saw their share of national posts dwindle astronomically. There was another twist to this story. Tigrayans used to have power and prestige. When they lost the throne after the death of Emperor Yohannes (who was from Tigray), to the upstart pretender from Shewa (Haile Selassie), they lost more than the throne. And then Haile Selassie started to reduce the sphere of influence and power held by the senior elite of the province. Their struggle seemed to be more about the restoration of Tigrayan rights, and recognition of their proper place in the world. Clearly, both northern provinces had reasons for their discontent.

But, their discontent was not my problem, or was it? In the first week of April 1991, my Amharic language teacher did not show up for my lesson. I called around to his other students to find out what happened. It turned out he was Eritrean and had gone "underground." Clearly the war and the rebels were coming closer to Addis. Eritreans in the capital must be feeling threatened if they had to "disappear." Now, I couldn't distinguish between Amhara and Eritrean ethnic groups, but through their names and their accents, Ethiopians would certainly be able to do so. I got the distinct feeling that if the war came to the capital, the confrontation would not be pretty.

Chapter 13

Uganda

I got another call from AFRO.

"Please go to Uganda to assist in identifying a suspected yellow fever case."

Why did I have this sense of impending doom? I didn't want to leave Ethiopia at this uncertain time, but it seemed like every country but Ethiopia was having an outbreak. What if the UN was ordered out of the country while I was consulting outside? I didn't want to leave my personal possessions at the Ghion, but I had to travel light. The afternoon sunlight cast a depressing hue on my dark-blue soft-sided travel bag thrown on the bed at the Ghion. My abdominal muscles were cramping, but they usually did before the start of a journey into the unknown. My mind refused to focus on the clothes to include on this trip. I still had to pick up my per diem for the trip from the office. Well, at least I could get some cash in dollars. Ethiopian birr were worthless outside the country. This time, I was prepared. I would locate my bag on the tarmac and watch them physically place it on the plane. I was flying via Nairobi to Entebbe where the WHO/Uganda country office jeep would meet me. It was a quick plane change in Nairobi on the way there, but on the return I had an overnight and could talk to the country office about meningitis.

Yellow fever (YF) is an acute viral hemorrhagic disease transmitted by infected mosquitoes. The "yellow" in the name refers to the jaundice that affects some patients. A small proportion of patients who contract the virus develop severe symptoms, and approximately half of those die within 7 to 10 days. Epidemics of yellow fever occurred when infected people introduced the virus into heavily populated areas with high mosquito density and where most people have little or no immunity, due to lack of vaccination. While foreigners needed the YF vaccination to enter Uganda, the local population was not vaccinated. Yellow fever was difficult to diagnose, especially during the early stages. There was no specific cure, but supportive care was crucial.

I was met at the airport by a WHO jeep that would take me directly to the concerned district hospital, after I met the WHO country office staff. After a short overview with WHO, I left immediately to connect with the rural district health officer in his office. He presented an overview of the patient's symptoms. When he arrived three days previously, he had a high fever, headache, nausea, and vomiting. He complained of muscle aches and pains, particularly in the abdomen, in the back, and around the knees. They initially thought of malaria, but his smears were all negative.

"Let's go over to the ward so I can see the patient," I said.

The infectious disease ward was empty, except for this patient lying under a mosquito net that covered the whole bed. We pulled up the mosquito net to observe the patient. He was awake and the first thing I noticed was that the sclerae of his eyes were a deep yellow. He had jaundice. He had an IV drip going into his left arm. His skin had a yellow cast to it. I felt an enlarged liver in his abdomen. He still had muscular aches and did not like me pounding his back over the kidneys.

"What about other tests?" I asked. The doctor responded that the urine specimen was bloody, and the liver enzymes were elevated. He said the patient came from a village near a forest. This patient had a history of going into the forest to hunt. He probably came into contact with mosquitoes that bred in the wild and fed on infected monkeys. While the YF virus could infect monkeys, it normally caused an asymptomatic illness that didn't kill them. As more people went into the forest for hunting or other work, increased human contact occurred with infected mosquitoes.

The doctor had ruled out malaria, and the case was doing satisfactorily clinically. His blood samples had already been sent to the viral lab in Entebbe, but we would have to wait several weeks to take additional ones to test for YF antibodies. He could also have leptospirosis, which had similar symptoms, but yellow fever was the more likely culprit. Leptospirosis also needed serological tests to determine the diagnosis. The patient's blood would be tested for antibodies for both diseases. At this juncture we needed to keep him isolated under a mosquito net on the infection diseases ward, to keep him sealed off from any mosquitoes in the locality. His family was under surveillance, and the village had been sprayed with insecticide—particularly around his house—for mosquitoes. If this were an outbreak in an urban center, vaccination of the population and mosquito control would have been key to prevention and control. It was not practical to spray wild mosquitoes in forest areas. The district had handled the diagnosis and treatment of this case correctly and had immediately notified authorities in the capital. I suspected that as more villagers went into the forest to augment their food supplies at home, clinics would be seeing more of these cases.

I wrapped up my investigation rapidly and headed back to Nairobi the following day. I hadn't heard anything on the radio about Ethiopia. I talked up meningitis control at the WHO/Kenya office, but they were more concerned about the location of the YF outbreak in Uganda and its distance from Kenyan borders. I was leaving on a flight back to Addis Ababa the following morning. But I had the afternoon free. Nairobi had many shopping attractions, from designer clothing boutiques to one-of-a-kind jewelry. But tourist shopping was not on my mind.

I couldn't get the evacuation of American nonessential staff and families from Addis out of my mind. It weighed on me, blocking out all other thoughts. My intuition told me to stock up on emergency supplies, since war was coming to the Ethiopian capital. So what happens in war, Connie? I fretted. Things shut down; banks, markets, and airports close. Addis was not a "Western capital." I doubted they even had baby formula or disposable diapers readily available. Best to buy these items here, now in Nairobi. But the Ministry hadn't even told me I was approved to look for a child. Wasn't I jumping the gun here? True, but the Girl Scout in me said, "Be prepared!"

The hotel receptionist gave me the tip. "Go to Biashara Street in downtown Nairobi; the stores are only about babies and children. You can find anything there."

And off I went. I suspected that the shopkeepers would want to know about my baby. How old was she, where was she born, and what was her name? To stave off questions, my cover was that I was picking up items for close friends in Addis. I bought clothes, cloth diapers, disposable diapers, and six large cans of baby formula and four baby bottles with nipples. This would certainly fill up my suitcase. But I swore to myself I wouldn't tell Monica about these purchases. She would think I was getting a little crazy.

I was back in Addis the next day, in time for the weekly EPR staff meeting. The current director of the EPR Centre was an

Egyptian named Dr. Suleiman. He started by briefing us on the situation of the war and that there was nothing alarming. The UN was staying in Ethiopia, including families and nonessential staff. He reminded staff that in an emergency our evacuation point was Nairobi, only three hours away. Then individual staff gave an update on the work they were doing.

Dr. Roma, involved in humanitarian issues, hesitantly said, "I don't want to bring up the evacuation of American families, but I don't think they would remove families if things didn't seem dire."

Our boss, Dr. Suleiman, replied, "The Americans always leave early, at the first hint of trouble. The UN stays to help people. There is no reason to be afraid." Then he mentioned he would be in Finland and Geneva in early May, and I would be acting director during his absence.

That effectively closed the meeting, and we all trooped out.

I had a bad feeling in my gut. It didn't seem like a good time for the director to be out of Addis.

A few short weeks later, on April 25, 1991, the US surprised us once again. It was authorizing the evacuation of all personnel except for essential staff. That meant six hundred Americans were leaving their posts! Dr. Suleiman told me he was still leaving for his conference on May 1, and we needed to go over office procedures. I couldn't believe he wasn't cancelling his trip.

That last weekend in April, I got a call from a friend in an NGO. She heard that a private house was available for rent in the area off the Debre Zeit Road. She gave me the telephone number of the owner. Now I was in a quandary. Technically, I had been waiting eight months to get assigned lodging and I still had not received any official notice. Would I ever get official lodging? And where were these rebels currently? Gonder was 450 miles by road from the capital. It would take months for the rebels to advance. If a house was available, I wanted out of the hotel. The grapevine claimed that a number of UN folk had arranged "private" lodging. The problem would arise only when I went to leave my post, because I would need to prove that no US dollars had exchanged hands and I would need receipts for my last two months' lodging in-country. Apparently, two to three months before leaving post, staff would move into a hotel so they had receipts for lodging. I thought I would call the landlord and go look at the house, and see how they interpreted the Proclamation on Private Property.

Chapter 14

Acting Director

As acting director now, I had to worry about the expatriate staff of the Centre along with the national staff of secretaries and drivers. If the situation on the ground were to change, I would be called to meet with other members of the UN Country Team. Now that the Americans were gone, it was so quiet in the halls of the ECA building which once were bustling with commotion. It was the quiet of the doomed, but I put on a positive demeanor since I was management now. This was a temporary assignment, and I could get through two to three weeks. In my office, the telephone pierced the eerie silence with a shrill, unsettling sound.

"Dr. Davis," came Werke's calm voice. "The committee has reviewed your documents and we approve your application to adopt. You may look for a child now!"

The breath was sucked out of my lungs and, for a second, I was speechless.

"Dr. Davis, are you there?"

"Yes, I just wasn't expecting this good news for a while. Thank you for calling!" I slowly put the receiver down.

As I stared out into space, I racked my brains. Now what do I do?

I picked up the phone and hurriedly dialed Monica.

"Werke told me I could look for a child. They approved me!"

"Congratulations, Connie!" Monica said.

"Great time to look for a baby," I complained. "The rebels are advancing. The Americans evacuated the rest of their staff. The director of the Centre decides it's a great time to travel and leaves me in charge!"

Then I laid out my plan going forward. I would go by Black Lion Hospital the next day to talk to the director of Pediatrics and to see the social workers posted in the emergency room. I asked Monica to contact her friends in NGOs that might hear of female babies available for adoption. I was hoping I wouldn't have to go the orphanage route, as that would add an additional layer of rules and fees onto the process. I guess my picking up the clothes and formula in Nairobi was not so crazy after all! But getting cleared to look for a child made up my mind about one thing. I would take the rental of the private house on Debre Zeit Road and start preparing for an infant. I'd take my chances on explaining to the government later. I did not want to be in the Ghion with a baby!

On the way to work the next day, I had the driver stop at Black Lion Hospital so I could see the director of Pediatrics.

"Dr. Naviat," I said. "I'm excited: the committee has approved my application to adopt! I can look for an infant!" And we walked down to the orphan ward. The six beds were completely empty. I had been here only a month before, and there had been three infants. They had been severely malnourished; two of the infants were male. It seemed strange there were no infants in the unit.

"Don't worry," said Dr. Naviat. "I have your phone number, and if we get an infant girl I will give you a ring."

I thanked him and told him I had also talked to the social workers in the emergency room. After he reassured me they would call if they got an infant girl, I headed to the office. Things were bustling because, beside my own work, I was supervising and answering questions for the expat staff. The mood was heavy. Everyone was concerned about the rebels reaching the capital, and when or whether we would be evacuated to Nairobi. I was also worried, but my worry had to do that if we had to evacuate, my looking for an infant would stop completely. After work I had an appointment to see the owner of the Debre Zeit house and gave the directions to the driver. We honked at the closed doors to the compound and the guard flung open the gates. He had been expecting us. A sizable landscaped garden fronted the stone house. That was unexpected! I was always surprised by what lay behind compound walls. A woman came out of the residence.

"I'm Ferkete," said the youthful-looking woman. "Let me show you around."

The house was in a quiet residential area. The eaves of the house extended out some two feet, providing shade. From the veranda, you overlooked a magnificent garden. A large living room boasted a fireplace. Two bedrooms each had attached bathrooms, and the master bedroom was quite large. The kitchen was located behind the living room, with an adjacent dining room. There were several servants' quarters in the back, located in the basement.

"I think you would be quite comfortable here," Ferkete said.

I had already explained to her over the telephone that I was adopting.

"But where will you go if I take the house?"

"If it's all right with you," she said, "I want to stay in one of the servants' quarters. I can move my things out of the master bedroom."

She explained that there was a bathroom and a small kitchenette in the basement. She was alone. Her parents were deceased and left her the house, and her husband was conscripted into the army. The rent was reasonable, but she did want it in dollars. She assured me she would keep out of my way. I had to keep the guard (an old family retainer), but his pay would be covered in the rent. Her explanation regarding the rental of private property was that this property was hers and she could invite "friends" to live with her. It seemed like a good deal in every respect. Someone would be on the property during the day when I was at work. And she could locate a maintenance man if we had any electrical or plumbing problems to resolve. I moved in the second week of May. My focus was on preparing the house for an imminent baby and seeing where I could find a crib and other items. I kept any thoughts of the encroaching rebel army at bay.

Chapter 15

A House with a View

It was so delightful to move from the Ghion and to have a house of my own. I loved the sculptured garden, but I had little time to relax in it. I was busy at work responding to questions from Geneva about the situation in Addis and going to other meetings as "acting" director of the WHO/EPR Centre.

The population heard little news about the progress of the war. This was an authoritative government. They told you what they wanted you to know, and if they were losing battles, that would be the last thing to be shared. However, suddenly long lines formed at petrol stations, indicating a shortage of fuel. Then a proclamation was issued stating that Ethiopian civilians were not to drive their private cars on the weekends. UN personnel, diplomats, and government vehicles were exempt from this restriction. Yet, no traffic in the city also gave an eerie feeling to the capital. A curfew was enforced. No one was to be on the streets after eleven o'clock at night. Socializing with friends on the weekend meant that if I was at a party, at 10:45 p.m. there would be an announcement to hop in your car *now* to get home on time, or sleep on that friend's floor. No one wanted to deal with soldiers who set up checkpoints at strategic crossroads to catch errant stragglers. With the curfew, it was highly likely you would end up in jail or have to bribe your way out of the mess.

UN management meetings said the US was deeply involved in facilitating peace talks in London with all rebel factions and the Ethiopian government officials. So did that mean the rebels would not invade the capital? Personally, I thought the so-called peace talks were far removed from the fighting and the rebels on the ground. I doubted anyone in Addis truly knew what was happening in London.

Chapter 16

Mengistu Flees
— May 22, 1991 —

Rumors were swirling left and right, and everyone was engrossed in trying to ascertain how far away the two major rebel groups were from the capital. The big news was that the Eritrean People's Liberation Front and the Tigray People's Liberation Front had joined forces. I think the correct phrase to use was "pandemonium in the streets." Residents were rushing to take their money out of banks and heading to Mercado, the huge market, to stock up on food. The general belief was that the capital would be besieged or worse.

Maryam, the EPR director's secretary, knocked on my office door.

"Dr. Davis, I've gotten calls from my family that the banks and the markets are being overrun. People are trying to get as much money as possible to buy supplies. It's not payday, but is there any possibility we could get an advance?"

"I don't know what the rules say, but let me call Geneva to ask their advice," I said. I quickly called the Head of Communicable Diseases in Geneva and explained that things were rapidly headed south. I asked permission to use whatever funds were in the petty cash account to provide advance funds to the Ethiopian staff. They readily agreed. Once I got off the phone, I called in the national staff and told them of Geneva's decision. Cash was limited, but I was able to give each staff member about the equivalent of 100 USD in birr. That could at least let them help their families stock up on *injera* flour and other staples.

Then we heard the most bizarre radio announcement! President Mengistu Haile Mariam and fifty of his family and most trusted advisors had fled the country for Zimbabwe. So now who was in charge? I was called into an emergency meeting of the Heads of Agencies. When I walked out of the meeting, I didn't know much more than before. I called all the staff and told them to go home and prepare themselves as best they could. They should stay alert and listen for any UN announcements. The streets were full of people madly rushing to buy supplies, and traffic was congested on the major roads.

When I arrived home, I went to check my grocery supplies. They were fairly meager as I had not had time to properly stock the shelves and the refrigerator. And it was impossible to even get near a grocery store. I had a couple of cans of Campbell's soup, so I opened one and heated it up on the stove. Definitely, tomorrow, grocery shopping was on my list of *Things to Do*. Surely some of the stores that catered to Westerners would still have supplies. Before going to bed I called Monica, but she had no more information on the situation than I did.

I was so tired, but sleep was eluding me. Normally, I fell off to sleep fairly quickly but the house was still an unknown enigma. The neighborhood, thankfully, was wonderfully quiet. It was my mind I could not still. I can look for a child, Werke said. But what does Mengistu fleeing the country bode for those of us entrapped in the capital? Who was in charge of the Ethiopian army? Does this mean the war was over? If the war was over, then I could continue working in Addis and continue looking for an infant. Stop thinking, Connie, just go to sleep.

Chapter 17

Statue Toppled

I slowly opened my eyes. Where was I? Right, I was in my new house off the Debre Zeit Road. It was May 23, one day after Mengistu left the country. I felt drugged, but that was only because I had tossed and turned all night. So this was what stress made you feel like. I glanced out the window and saw the car was already there. No time to worry about what the day would bring. Maryam was already in the office when I arrived.

"Maryam, who is in charge of the government now that Mengistu has fled?"

"Apparently, Mengistu's former defense minister, Tesfaye Gebre-Kidan, is now running things. He's called a unilateral ceasefire and is asking the rebels not to advance to the capital and to wait for the peace talks scheduled to begin in five days."

I headed down the hall to check on the expat staff. They were all in their offices early, which was not the usual case.

"I don't have any new information to give you guys," I said.

I headed back to my office and turned on the computer. Maybe I could get some work done. Then, suddenly, a muffled roar began in the distance. I looked out my window, but I didn't have a direct view of the street below, so I hurriedly walked to the secretaries' office. Both secretaries were glued to the windows. The noise was much louder now, and you could see masses of people rushing down the street headed towards Meskal Square, towards the ECA building. The rabble completely filled the street and was composed mostly of adult men but interspersed here and there were the white shammas of several women. What in the world was going on? Revolution in the streets already?

I hurried back to my office and called Monica. Somehow, she always got the news faster than I did.

"The rumor here is that the new boss in town wants to distance himself from the former president. Seems they're going to tear down Lenin's statue. That's where everyone is headed."

Overnight, the government is distancing itself from Marxist-Leninist thought? This was unbelievable. I dashed back to the office where my WHO colleagues were gathered. They also were fixated on the last dregs of the mob that had descended towards the square. Suddenly, a monumental roar and chanting erupted. We couldn't see the square from our building, but we could hear the commotion and the chanting in Amharic which was later translated for us—*Mengistu thief, Lenin thief!* Maryam came running in and shouted that huge cranes had arrived at the square and put ropes around the bronze statue of Lenin to topple it. You could feel the excitement of the crowd, which gave up an epic roar at each frantic pull of the cranes. You could hear the thumping jackhammers attacking the concrete base trying to dislodge it. Along with the racket of the crowd roaring, you could clearly discern thousands of Ethiopians "trilling their tongues," which is a traditional way Ethiopians show glee. The noise overall was deafening. I didn't know whether to be terrified or exhilarated.

I could barely hear the high-pitched ring of the phone in my office. I sprinted back to my office and grabbed the phone. "Hello?"

Statue Toppled | 79

It was Geneva and I was given a high-priority task that needed to be executed immediately! WHO/Geneva had heard rumors the new government might release political prisoners. Our EPR Centre here had been working with Amnesty International to try and obtain the release of a former WHO secretary, Mebrahetu Gennet, who was the spouse and widow of the former Army Chief of Staff implicated in the assassination and coup attempt against Mengistu in May of 1989. Unfortunately, it was a *failed* coup attempt. And Mengistu summarily killed all nine generals involved. Mengistu's vengeance had a long reach, and he threw spouses and family members into jail even though they had no inkling of the coup attempt. For the last eighteen months, WHO had been pleading with the Ethiopian government to release Mebrahetu and her young daughter from prison, to no avail.

I immediately had Maryam call the head of the United Nations Development Programme (UNDP) and ask for an immediate audience. He told me to come right over. I explained the call from Geneva. He was aware of past endeavors by the EPR director to free Mebrahetu.

"You're in luck," he said. "A UN delegation is leaving shortly to meet the new provisional government task force on other matters. You can join them."

I raced back to the EPR Centre to get Maryam to type out a letter spelling the full name of Mebrahetu and her daughter and asking for their release. And then I joined the compact delegation and was given the opportunity to speak first.

"Sir, the name Mebrahetu Gennet is not unknown to your government. She and her young daughter have been falsely imprisoned for more than eighteen months in connection with the coup attempt against the former president. She was just a secretary in the WHO/EPR Centre. Her husband was a general, but she and her minor daughter are innocent. WHO/Geneva urgently requests that you release Ms. Gennet for medical evacuation to Geneva on humanitarian grounds. WHO will provide all the arrangements to evacuate her and her daughter. They may need passports issued urgently for their travel. Please consider this as the highest priority. Thank you."

The government official took the letter and indicated that he would look into the matter. I made a slight bow of the head and rapidly exited the conference room. I had no idea if the plea would be successful.

I made it back safely to the office, avoiding the mob scene around Lenin's statue, and called Geneva and let them know what had occurred. I couldn't know the outcome, but I thought Geneva should work on getting plane tickets for two people to leave within forty-eight hours. If the government was going to grant the request, it would likely come quickly. We needed to be ready. I would keep them apprised of all matters.

I didn't know it then, but the new provisional government had a lot of more serious items on their plate that day. Some 14,310 Ethiopian Jews (the Falashas, or Bete Isra'el, that I had met in Gonder in 1989) had been quietly massing in the Shola district outside Addis. Starting the next day, the Israeli government would *secretly* airlift them out of the country. Locals did not have any inkling about the airlift until the group arrived in Israel and it was *Breaking News* on the global stage the following day.

In the meantime, Maryam was in contact with relatives of Mebrahetu and alerted them to our efforts. It was late in the afternoon, and I was packing up to leave the office, when Maryam came running into my office.

"They released her! They released her and her daughter!" she cried.

Apparently some of the family had gone to the prison to wait, on the off chance that she would walk out. They were weak, but Mebrahetu wanted to take up Geneva's offer to leave. I dropped my briefcase and went to the computer to rush off an email to Geneva. Free at last! The provisional government released 187 political prisoners that day. I was only interested in two of them. We had work to do.

Chapter 18

UN Evacuation
— May 24, 1991 —

After another sleepless night, I walked into the office on May 24 and thought I would be working on Mebrahetu's imminent departure. But Maryam waylaid me in the hallway and said, "Dr. Davis, UNDP has called an urgent meeting of all Heads of Agencies today at 9am. I've already told the driver."

As I joined the select group in UNDP's conference room, an expectant hush settled over the gathering. The UN Resident Coordinator walked briskly into the room and wasted no words.

"The diplomatic community had a meeting with the new provisional government yesterday. Although the Ethiopian government declared a unilateral ceasefire, apparently the rebels are not in agreement. They are still advancing. I won't mince words: if the Tigrayan rebels enter the city, we expect to have a bloodbath," he said. I assumed this was payback for all the times the Amhara people lorded it over the Tigrayans.

"The airport will be the first thing to close down. The UN is to evacuate all employees except for a minimal staff of essential personnel starting tomorrow! I need a list of all staff members and their families' names by twelve noon, so we can calculate how many charter planes are needed. Each person can take one small suitcase. There will probably not be time for your admin personnel to prepare per diems, so contact your agency in Nairobi to request their assistance in supplying funds to your staff. I do not know when people will be able to return. They need to make arrangements with their domestic staff before they leave. Again, I need the list of personnel and family members before noon! Thank you for your cooperation."

As soon as I got back to the office, I called a meeting of all staff—both expat and national—to relay the news calmly. I was bombarded with questions. When would we be leaving? When could we return? Would the EPR Centre stay open? They were all legitimate questions, and I wished I had a crystal ball. I could only relay that the evacuation started the next day and Nairobi was the destination, so as soon as the briefing was over they needed to go home to pack a *small* bag. I didn't know when they could return.

"You need to take your personal computers and documents with you, so you can work in Nairobi. It would be prudent to plan on being out of Addis for at least a month. The UN will be coordinating everything in Nairobi and WHO will provide your per diems. They will tell you where you will sleep tomorrow night!" I ended by saying, "We don't know what to expect when the rebels enter the city. But I don't want any women or children to be here. I'll be working with the UN Coordinator to get all expat women in the EPR Centre out on the first planes. That includes our director's wife and four daughters, since he's at the conference in Finland."

As Maryam was leaving the meeting, I asked her to get Mrs. Suleiman on the phone. War was never good for women, so I knew she and the girls—aged two to sixteen years—needed to be on the first flight out. Maryam connected me to Mrs. Suleiman and I quickly brought her up to date. I stressed that she didn't have a lot of time, but to pack one small bag for each family member. I would not have per diems for them, but WHO in Nairobi was alerted and would have funds on arrival. I would call her back when I knew the flight time and when the driver would come to pick them up.

All she said was, "I'll call my husband now to tell him about the evacuation order."

Maryam came into my office with the evacuation list, and at the top were the names of Dr. Suleiman's family. I made a special request to get them out on the very first flight.

"Great, Maryam. This looks complete. Let's send this off to UNDP." I felt relieved, because now things seemed to be organized and under control.

Then Maryam brought me up to date on the status of travel for Mebrahetu and daughter. Their passports were being updated at Immigration as we spoke. And Geneva had sent the tickets already for their flight to Geneva on May 25. Great, it seemed everything was in order for them. So I had best sit down now and send off a message to Geneva about post evacuation. This had not been in the works. My thought was that I would stay on and keep the WHO/EPR Centre open. Besides, it was when things started to fall apart that an infant was most likely to be orphaned. I needed to stay in Addis.

And then in the afternoon, the Ethiopian radio announced some startling news: the new provisional government was looking for high-level officials and armed forces personnel from the ousted military government, and therefore no Ethiopians could leave the country! This new proclamation had an immediate chilling effect on certain UN families. A number of UN personnel were married with Ethiopian spouses and had biracial children. In some of these families the wives and children had dual passports, but most did not. The provisional government refused to lift the proclamation for the UN. These UN personnel were reluctant to leave their spouses, and therefore requested to stay behind. By UN accounts, they had a total of fifteen hundred personnel and family members to evacuate to Nairobi, minus those who requested to stay behind. Finding adequate numbers of charter planes was going to be a problem. And then in the late afternoon, I got an unsettling call from Mrs. Suleiman.

"Hello, Dr. Davis," she said. "I've spoken to my husband and he says you Americans are too ready to leave Addis, and that there's no problem. So we will stay."

At first I was stunned, and then I was angry.

"Mrs. Suleiman, your husband is not here and is not able to judge the situation. What's more, it's not the Americans who have ordered the evacuation; this is the UN, and all families and nonessential staff members are to leave for Nairobi. I just received notice that you and your girls are on the first plane out tomorrow. Do I have to remind you what happens to women in war? It's not pretty."

"I'm sorry, Dr. Davis, but my husband says we're not to leave."

"Let me be clear here, Mrs. Suleiman. When the rebels enter the city, and the bombs are dropping all around, it will be too late to call for help. It will be too dangerous for anyone to attempt to help you. Please, reconsider!"

And I slammed down the phone. I guess I handled that diplomatically. I was fuming. If you were not worried for yourself, at least think about your sixteen-year-old. Sexual assaults are a well-known weapon of war, and being a diplomat would not save you or your family. Well, I tried my best. I needed to give this information to the evacuation committee, so others could be put on the plane. No one was going to be happy about this.

I started calling the EPR expat staff to give them their times to be at the airport. I told them the time the car would be picking them up, but they should be ready and outside the door to load suitcases quickly. They seemed composed. At this point, you could only hope you got out before the airport was shut down. I was preparing to head home when the landline jangled once again. Damn, now who was calling me? I grabbed the phone.

"Hello."

It was Geneva calling.

"Dr. Davis, we've made a decision. You need to close down the office and evacuate with the rest of the staff to Nairobi."

I laughed and shook my head. "What? That's what everyone told me WHO would do!"

The Communicable Disease Chief asked, "What do you mean? I don't understand."

"When I first arrived in Addis and was making the rounds to UN offices, introducing myself, I was roundly questioned about the 'purpose' of the WHO/EPR *Emergency* Centre. They told me that at the first hint of trouble WHO would round up all staff and evacuate to safety. I guess they were right."

Silence on the other end. And then I proposed a solution.

"Look, let me keep the Centre open. I can assess what's needed after the rebels storm the city. I can write whatever appeal is necessary, and the EPR staff can get paid at the end of the month."

Silence again on the other end. "Fine, Connie, you can stay."

I replaced the phone in its cradle and took a deep breath. I sat there letting the enormity of the situation sink into my brain. I had just volunteered to stay in a war zone because my intuition was telling me to stay.

Chapter 19

Rebels Capture Asmara

I arrived at the office quite early on May 25, 1991, in order that both SUV cars could be dedicated to picking up and ferrying their passengers to the airport. This was going to be a long day. Maryam greeted me right away.

"Did you hear the radio announcement?"

I shook my head, no.

"Eritrean rebels have captured Asmara!" she said.

I hoped everyone could get on the airplanes before the airport was shut down. If the rebels had taken Asmara, that meant the last Ethiopian government fortress in the north of the country had fallen. Events would likely proceed rapidly.

The UN and other Western powers were evacuating their staff. The Americans had evacuated all but essential staff two months ago. In hindsight, I'm sure the UN wished they had joined the Americans at that moment. Western employees who had Ethiopian spouses were in a particularly stressful situation. Both EPR vehicles were still at the airport. Only the secretaries were in the front office. With the expat staff gone, they were at loose ends. I suggested it was a good time to do an inventory of the Centre's equipment and supplies. Best to verify what was in place before the rebel occupation.

I thought Mrs. Suleiman would recant her foolhardy choice to remain, but the office phone remained mute, as if the incoming invading forces had already cut all communication lines. Then I saw an email from the UN Resident Coordinator. Tigrayan rebels were twelve miles from the capital. Fear. Maryam came into my office with the report that Mebrahetu and daughter navigated the special chaos that was always at Immigration. They were accompanied by a special escort and were on the plane for Frankfurt and then Geneva. Relief.

"Good news," I said. "I'll send an email to Geneva right now."

I wondered how the EPR expat staff were progressing. The second driver had not returned. The truth was, I hated being the person left behind. I would rather be the first person to volunteer for a dangerous assignment than the last person in a secure bunker. Why was that? I guess that waiting is so *passive*. The ones who had left were the active ones; they were scrambling to contact family and alert them to the evacuation. There was also the excitement of the unknown, like wondering what the next day would bring. We had two rebel armies hell bent on being the first to reach the capital to claim the spoils. I was in the wrong place at the wrong time. I looked way too Ethiopian for my own good. I wondered if the rebels could distinguish that I was American, not Ethiopian.

Then I heard a commotion in the secretaries' office. The second driver had returned.

"Dr. Davis, the airport is shut down!" the driver said. "Dr. Roma was left behind. I took her back to her apartment."

This was not a good sign.

Damn, and things had been so rushed that I didn't have time to say goodbye to Monica before her departure to Nairobi.

Chapter 20

Call Sign WHISKEY

Maryam greeted me on arrival at the office with a terse message.

"All UN essential staff are to meet at the UNDP conference room at nine o'clock today," she said.

I left at once!

As I looked around the conference room to see if I knew anyone, I heard a familiar voice.

"Hey, Connie, sit over here," Monica called.

I rushed over to join her, whispering, "You didn't go to Nairobi?"

"I'll tell you all about it when the meeting is over," she murmured.

The UN Resident Coordinator breezed in with several burly, serious-looking men. He quickly launched into a synopsis of the evacuation of staff. Unfortunately, about one hundred staff members could not get on a charter plane before they shut down the airport. The UN was working with authorities to have it reopened as soon as possible. He now turned the meeting over to the UN Security men that had accompanied him, to explain how essential staff would be alerted to key messages. The security detail started to pass out two-way radios. Everyone issued a walkie-talkie was identified as essential staff and should guard their radio. We were entrusted to pass messages on by landline to those UN staff who could not get on the charters. There were a limited number of radios. He then proceeded to read each staff member's name and to give them their call sign.

"Dr. Connie Davis, your call sign is WHISKEY," he said, and continued on down the list.

Several people snickered at the call sign. I wondered why they gave me this call sign?

The radio was a black, two-pound eight-by-three-by-two-inch monstrosity, with an antenna that added an additional four inches to the length. I had a medium-size purse, and no way could I fit this radio in. So I would have to put it in my beat-up brown leather briefcase, which would present other problems. My purse was always with me, in any emergency. The briefcase, more than likely, normally sat on a chair next to my desk. It held important papers and a few lunch tidbits, and it seldom moved positions. I never played with those toy walkie-talkies as a child, so I needed to pay attention to the instructions.

For starters, the radio was always tuned to a particular channel for the UN. You needed to keep it recharged. It was everyone's responsibility to memorize call signs. Do not respond if it's not your call sign. Interrupt only for an emergency. And remember—no sensitive or confidential information transmitted by radio, because everyone can hear you! A booklet came with the radio, but he went over the basic radio etiquette rules. The important ones were:

Roger	You received and understood the message.
Come in	You are asking the other party to acknowledge they hear you.

Copy	You understand what was said.
Wilco	You will comply.
Over	Your message is finished.
Out	Your conversation is finished. The channel is clear for others to use.

That evening we were instructed to read all the instructions and to get comfortable with the radio. We needed to keep the radio close. It would advise if we could come to work or should stay at home. It was our lifeline. If we had a real shortwave radio at home, we should listen to the BBC for news updates. Hmm, no shortwave radio with me. The landlines, probably, would continue to work.

They passed out more goodies for the assembly. We each received a rolled-up poster, which they proceeded to show us. It was a large three-by-two-foot poster with a red background and black Amharic scripts. Roughly translated, it was supposed to say—DO NOT ENTER! THIS HOUSE BELONGS TO A DIPLOMAT. We were to tack the poster up on the front door of our house. Security assured us that expatriates would likely not be targeted. The fight was between Ethiopians. I wondered how many rebels—who had lived in the bush for the last ten years—knew how to read Amharic!

As we trooped out of the conference hall, I turned to Monica and said, "How did you stay behind?"

"Turns out the WHO country office director has dependent children and needed to leave with them. She asked for a volunteer to stay to keep the country office open, since the WHO/EPR Centre was to remain open. Didn't want to leave you solo, Connie."

When I got back to the EPR Centre, I called a meeting of the local staff. The next days were important, so keep tuned in to the national radio. If the rebels were to enter the city, everyone should stay home. I notified staff that I would borrow one of the EPR cars to drive myself to and from work. This way, the driver did not have to be out in the street so much. Not to worry. I knew how to drive.

I might know how to drive, but it was touch and go about whether I knew how to find my way home the first time. It's just that, once I left the main road, there were no road signs and I had to remember the way.

I made it home with no wrong turns. I carried the two-way radio into my bedroom and plugged in the receiver. It certainly was quiet; even the radio was silent. I wanted to vegetate before the fireplace, but I was fading fast. I didn't know what the next day would bring, and I was nervous about the rebels poised to enter the city. We all hoped last-minute peace efforts would protect the capital from invasion. I ate leftover chili from the late lunch I had eaten. I barely had time for a quick shower before I fell into bed. I checked to make sure I had set the alarm. And then I was out.

Chapter 21

Emergency

It was strange driving myself to work the next day. Practically no one was on the roads. The diplomats had advised the rebels to give the peace talks in London a chance, but I wasn't sure rebels on the ground had any trust in London. Right now, it was up to the rebels. They could show restraint, or charge headstrong into the city. I hoped for the former, but I was preparing for the latter.

I arrived early to work. My radio was sticking out of my briefcase and making hissing sounds, but that was it. I stuck my head in the secretaries' office to let Maryam know I was around. I threw my briefcase on the chair by the desk and opened my computer, to learn that UNICEF would be reporting on various refugee camps in Ethiopia. I should probably attend to get an update on the health status of refugees. And I had best get going, since their offices were located in another part of the city. I grabbed my purse and rushed out the door.

I didn't return to the EPR office until after two in the afternoon. The landline was ringing.

"Connie, where have you been?" Monica asked.

"I was in meetings all morning. What's up?"

"You didn't have your radio with you," Monica said. "And boy did you miss an announcement. An emergency call went out over the radio from the American Embassy. They were looking for a doctor or other health personnel who could volunteer to go between the opposing warring armies to rescue a family in Debre Zeit. Apparently, the family was fleeing for Addis, but their vehicle was caught in the crossfire. They have a nine-month-old infant who was shot when the SUV came under fire," Monica explained. "I waited to see if anyone volunteered. Or if you were listening. Nothing. So I said I was sure you'd go, that you were a pediatrician, and I'd track you down on your landline."

"So, Monica, let me get this straight. You volunteered me to cross enemy lines to provide first aid to some insane family that hesitated too long to get to safety in Addis?" I queried.

Silence. "Yeah, it kind of slipped out," she said.

Great, I don't even have to be present and I get volunteered.

"I'll call the embassy and find out more details," I said.

I wondered what the family was doing in Debre Zeit. In fact, what were they doing in Ethiopia at all? I thought all Americans had long departed some two months ago. Well, the only way to find out was to call the US Embassy. I supposed the consular officer would know the situation.

"Hello, this is Dr. Connie Davis. I heard you were looking for a doctor. What's up?" I asked.

"Thank you for calling," said Mike, the consular officer. He then proceeded to give me the details. The family in question worked for the International Livestock Research Institute (ILRI), which was an independent research institute. Its mission was to improve food and nutritional security by identifying efficient, safe, and sustainable use of livestock. Various partners funded the institute. Patricia Williams was a US citizen, and John Williams—who worked for ILRI—was from the United

Kingdom. Although the main campus of ILRI was on the outskirts of the northeast side Addis, he had been doing research in Debre Zeit. They initially thought they would stay where they were, but then got frightened as the rebels got closer to Addis. They waited too long to try to return to Addis. "They were in the wrong place, at the wrong time," said Mike. Their SUV was riddled with bullets and they returned to Debre Zeit—where they noticed their son was shot through the baby seat, which was in the back seat of the car. He was not doing well.

"Dr. Davis, the embassy normally has a doctor on contract to provide care for all our employees. But I guess he felt that, as an Eritrean, he had best go underground until things calm down. He quit his duties two days ago," Mike said.

The consular officer continued to talk about the well-equipped medical unit in the embassy, which included an ambulance and a six-bed mini hospital.

"We have everything but personnel. And that's why we sent out the message. Are you willing to go? The parents will be overjoyed. But it will be risky," Mike said. "We'd like the ambulance to leave ASAP, but security is checking out the roads. I'll call you later tonight to let you know whether it's a go."

"I'll go," I said. "Give me their telephone number in Debre Zeit so I can call the Williamses."

I thought I would head home early to rest up and prepare for who knew what. But before I could leave the office, the phone rang again. This time it was from the UN Resident Coordinator.

"Connie, my staff told me about the US Embassy radio appeal. You do not work for the Americans. You are UN staff! What they are asking you to do is dangerous!"

"I know it's risky, but if I were a parent in that situation, I would like someone to come help me. So, I'm going."

And we hung up. I barely could open the front door of

my rental house before the phone was ringing off the hook. I grabbed it.

It was the consular officer.

"Security said fighting was intense on the road leading into Addis. The ambulance can't go tomorrow. The rebels will be in the capital by then," he said. "I'll call the family."

I didn't know whether to be relieved or depressed. My phone call to the parents would be difficult, but best to get it over.

"Hello, Mrs. Williams, this is Dr. Connie Davis. How are you guys doing?"

She broke down crying. "We were praying you were coming tomorrow," she said. "The nurse associated with the Tigrayan rebels came by tonight. He looked at the wound, said he didn't know how to treat such a small infant, and left."

They had initially gone to the closest health center—an X-ray was taken showing a bullet in his lower back, at lumber vertebra 4.

"Baby John's not moving his lower limbs."

Then I asked, "Is he drinking fluids, and can he pee?"

"Yes, he is peeing, and he is taking his bottle," Patricia said.

"OK, Mom, listen closely. It's very important to try and encourage him to take fluids. We need to keep him hydrated. I'll come as soon as the embassy gives the OK. You have to stay strong now. I'll call again tomorrow." And I hung up.

Tomorrow Addis would be under siege. How would that go? I knew some UN staff with family had checked into the Hilton, thinking it might offer additional security. I picked up the poster and tacked it up on the front door with tape I had brought from the office. Then I closed the door with the dead bolt. I needed to think about Plan B if the rebels went street-by-street, house-to-house. What would they be looking for? Mengistu's soldiers? Money? I stopped before my train of thought got to women.

Now, what would make me *not* look Ethiopian? I would have five seconds to make my case.

I slouched down in a sofa chair in the living room and closed my eyes. My mind flickered back to Somalia 1980. I had been leading a small team of three epidemiologists from the Centers for Disease Control/Atlanta. We had arrived in Mogadishu before the start of a nutritional survey of Ethiopian refugees who had sought refuge in Somali UN camps. The US Congress had questioned journalists' reports of severe malnutrition and were loath to approve food aid. So the Centers for Disease Control and Prevention was requested to conduct a nutritional survey. Our team was heading off in two days to three different areas in Ethiopia to conduct the surveys. We would be gone for a month and living under trying circumstances, so we wanted to relax, hear some music, and de-stress before leaving. UN officials had told us about several discothèques in the capital, and we had gone to dinner and dancing.

Whenever I'm assigned to a new place, I like to explore the food and national dress. The Somali women were stunning, and they wore these A-line dresses with diaphanous, multicolored material coming from Yemen. Most Somali women did not wear burkas in those days, despite Somalia being a Muslim country. I had a tailor make up a dress in two hours and thought I'd wear it out to dinner to "look Somali." I was walking home with my two male team members from the disco around eleven o'clock. We had stopped in front of the Russian Embassy, looking at some photos and laughing about something. In the distance, I heard and felt the rumble of a huge military truck coming down the street. We looked up and wondered what it was doing slowly creeping down the street. I suddenly got a terrible feeling in my stomach. The truck screeched to a halt, and two soldiers jumped down with drawn assault rifles.

I stepped forward and shouted, "You are making a big *fucking* mistake. I am *not* Somali! So get right back on that truck and keep on going!"

My male companions stared at me speechless!

"Sorry, sorry," said one of the soldiers and motioned to the other one to back up. They jumped into the cab of the military truck and they sped off down the street.

"What the hell was that?" yelled my colleague Ron.

"You are not going to believe this!" I told them about this private briefing I had right before leaving for Somalia with Dr. Wolfe Bulle, a well-known humanitarian who worked for thirty years with various NGOs. He had put together briefing packets for different Asian and African countries, as to the cultural and religious sensitivities one needed to work in other cultures. The Centers for Disease Control and Prevention sent a lot of epidemiologists out to work on outbreaks, and the briefing documents were to help people "new" to disaster situations be prepared to cope with the inevitable culture clash.

Lab and infectious disease specialists had briefed us as to the diseases we would encounter. We also discussed at length how we would conduct the nutritional survey and the methodology. So I had no clue as to why Wolfe wanted to see me.

"Connie, I know you have the briefing packet on Somalia so you can read up on particular customs at your leisure. I just wanted to alert you to something fairly new that won't be in the briefing material," Dr. Bulle said. "I recently heard something from a friend who just got back from a UN assignment in Somalia."

And then he proceeded to tell me some worrisome information.

"What I'm going to say would not pertain to a white woman epidemiologist going over there, but you know you look like a Somali woman."

The UN and various Western NGOs have been in Somalia addressing the humanitarian situation. And I guess Western men have appreciated the beauty of the Somali women and have been going out with them. Apparently, the Somali government—which was conservative and Muslim—was not happy "their" women were seeing foreign men. They couldn't exactly kick out Western aid, because they did need it. They couldn't exactly beat up the men, which might cause an international scene. But they could put pressure on their women. The military was going around late at night, and if they saw a Somali woman out with a Westerner, they picked her up, tossed her into a truck, and took her to jail. After a five-day stay in jail, harassment, and a little beating, the women were warned not to continue to go out with foreigners, or else . . .

"Just be careful. Stay alert."

I thanked Bulle for the heads up.

"So, when that military truck started down the street," I told my companions, "I knew there would be a confrontation. I had five seconds to make them believe I was American and back off! Fortunately, they did!"

Here I was, in Ethiopia, again looking just like a local! But in Addis Ababa in 1991, few Ethiopian women wore pants—or denim blue jeans. Those who worked in Western embassies might wear a straight skirt and blouse. Standard dress was still the traditional *habesha kemis*—the cotton cloth called *shemma*, which was woven in long vertical sheets and then sewn together to make a dress, usually with embroidery around the hem. So the following day, I knew I needed to wear US attire—denim jeans with a T-shirt, hair in a ponytail, and my red Western bandana tied around my head in the back. I would definitely look different. Would it be enough to save my life?

Chapter 22

The Rebels
— May 28, 1991 —

I woke with a start. It was the noise—loud, pounding, persistent, and scary. I didn't need a warning from the radio to tell me the rebels were bombing the city. The phone rang, and I picked up the receiver.

"Are you awake?" Monica asked.

"I am now," I said. "This is going to be a long day."

I dressed quickly in jeans and T-shirt and padded around in bare feet. I scanned the house, trying to determine how to make it appear more secure. I would leave the outside wooden shutters closed. I wandered through the rooms to find the corner furthest from a window. The master bedroom faced the front garden and had numerous windows to catch the light. Not the safest place to hide when the bombs dropped closer to the house. The guest bedroom faced the back of the house and looked down on a utility area and the compound's nine-foot-tall walls. Two medium-sized windows adorned the room. There was a double bed and a walk-in closet. Yes, if things got bad, I could huddle behind the mattress in the closet for safety.

No one tells you what to do while waiting for an advancing army. My orientation in Brazzaville a year earlier had laid out the goals for meningitis prevention and control, but no helpful tips for calming the mind for a bombardment. I made coffee. The caffeine kept me alert. The noise from the bombing got louder yet seemed farther away. I surmised that the rebels must be targeting the Palace area, which had a large contingent of government forces. Good thing I lived east of the Palace, about two miles away. Then my telephone rang again. I ran to the living room to answer it.

"Hello, Dr. Davis?" I could barely hear the voice for all the background rocket noise and children crying. "This is Mrs. Suleiman."

I had completely forgotten about Dr. Suleiman's family.

"Our house is in an unfortunate area near the Palace. The Palace is under constant bombardment. I don't know what to do. We have to get out of here," she cried.

I screamed into the phone, "I can hardly hear you for the noise. Tell me, do you have an inner room in the house with few or no windows? Grab pillows or a mattress and take all the children into this room. Get down on the floor. Huddle under the mattress. I'll contact the emergency team, but no one can come now. It's too dangerous."

I dialed the emergency number for the UN.

"Hello, this is Connie Davis. Dr. Suleiman's family apparently lives close to the Palace. There is fierce fighting in the area. They need to be evacuated from their house," I said.

I heard a few choice words. They made it clear that no one could move at this time. Once the shelling had stopped, the UN team would attempt to come get them.

I called Mrs. Suleiman. "I contacted the UN emergency team. Once the shelling has stopped and they think it's safe, they'll come for you. Hang tight, they will come."

I couldn't help but think they could have been safe and sound in Nairobi. Now someone would risk their life for them. I could only hope the battle ended quickly. Now was a waiting game. The battle continued for several hours. I must have fallen asleep on the floor of the rental guest room, covered with blankets I pulled off the bed. It was the silence that woke me. Finally, relief! No more rockets and the whine of bullets. It was almost one in the afternoon. I called the UN emergency number.

They had already sent a UN vehicle for Mrs. Suleiman and her girls.

"Don't worry, Dr. Davis. We know the address. We'll take them to the Hilton, where other families have moved."

The UN radio told us to continue sheltering in place. Sporadic fighting continued around the city. Sometime later in the evening, the phone jangled again.

"Hello, Connie," said the consular officer. "Since the rebels are in the capital, we think it will be OK to send the ambulance to Debre Zeit tomorrow."

However, they thought it too dangerous for me to come this evening to the embassy to go to the medical stores for supplies.

"Tell me what you need," said Mike, the consular officer.

And I proceeded to list a gamut of supplies including butterfly needles, IV sets, gloves, antibiotics, syringes and needles, alcohol and other antiseptic supplies, tape, and any and all pediatric supplies.

"Put them in the ambulance, and I'll sort through them later in Debre Zeit," I said. Then I told him where I lived.

"The ambulance will be at your house at seven in the morning."

I called the Williams family.

"I'm coming tomorrow for sure!"

Davis Family circa 1995 right before Connie is posted to India a 2nd time as Resident Coordinator UNAIDS. **Top row from Left to Right:** Donald M. Millar,* (college roommate of Colbert), Cheryl Cook Davis, (wife of Colbert S. Davis III), Briana Toi Jeanne Wong Davis (daughter of Ed and Cynthia), Cynthia Wong Davis, (wife of Edward), Edward Henry Davis (younger brother of Connie), Colbert S. Davis III, (older brother of Connie), **Lower row from Left to Right:** Author Cornelia E Davis MD (Connie), Colbert S. Davis IV, (Colby, son of Colbert III), Dr. Colbert S. Davis II, MD, (Head of the Davis clan), Cornelia Louise McNeal Davis, (Spouse of Dr. Colbert Davis), Rachel Elizabeth Davis (daughter of Colbert-older brother), and Romene Alaana Davis, (daughter of Connie Davis).

You may wonder how Don Millar got in this photo? Grandma Davis always invited him to Sunday dinner since he didn't have any "family" in the Bay Area.

Mushroom Cloud Explosion of a secret underground munitions depot by retreating Mengistu soldiers Addis Ababa June 5, 1991. *Photo by Mark Thomas* UNICEF Photographer Note, this photo is on the front cover.

Rebel Hats Party at Monica's apartment celebrating surviving the Rebel takeover of the capital and receiving the maroon colored hats of the Rebel Army.

Dr. Connie Davis leaving Black Lion Hospital with her daughter Romene Alaana. June 17, 1991.
Photo by Monica Wernette

Monica with Romene: Romene with her Godmother Monica.
Photo by Connie Davis

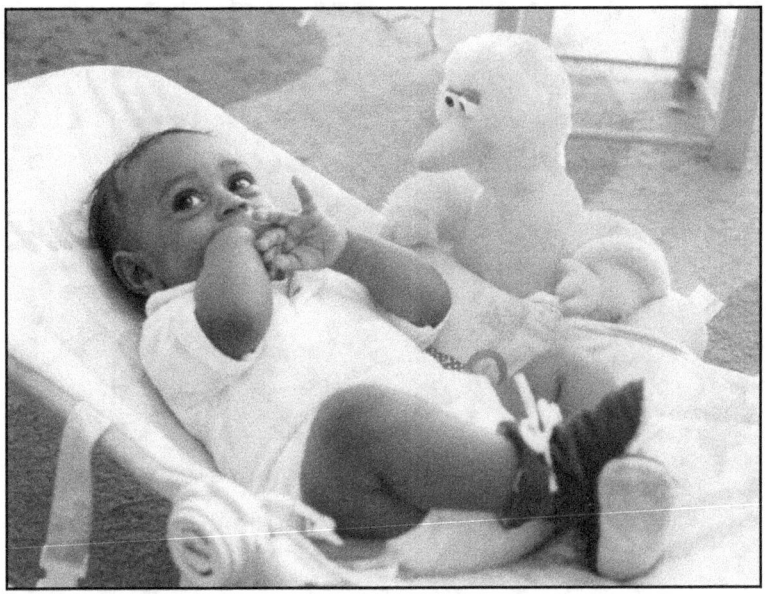

Romene at five months old up in the mountains at Kirkwood CA.

Coffee Ceremony: Connie preparing the coffee ceremony at Romene's Christening party.

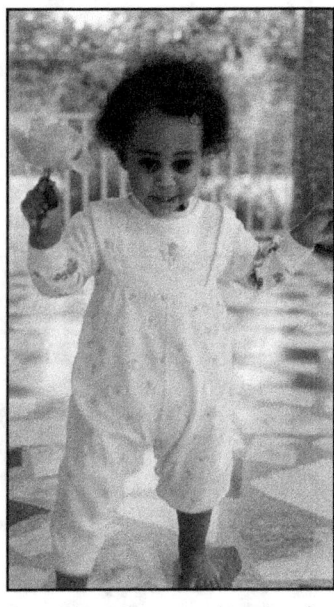

First Steps: Romene taking her first steps at 13 months old on the porch of the house in Old Airport neighborhood.
Photo by Monica Wernette

Lalibela One of the monolithic churches at Lalibela, UNESCO World Heritage site. *Photo by Connie Davis*

Priest. One of the guardian priests at Lalibela. *Photo by Connie Davis*

Chapter 23

Debre Zeit

The ambulance was at my house at seven in the morning. I was ready and hopped in the front seat.

"Hi, I'm Dr. Davis," I said.

"My name is Amare," the ambulance driver said.

And we were off. The plan I discussed with the consular officer was to go directly to the Williamses' house in Debre Zeit. Once I had stabilized the child, we would return directly to the embassy medical unit. The health unit was well equipped, and the embassy compound included a room where I could stay, so it wasn't necessary for me to go back and forth.

It was as eerily quiet as midnight in a cemetery when the ambulance headed out of town. I wondered if we would cross roadblocks as we left the city. I felt fairly confident, and not afraid. I was in an ambulance, clearly marked with these huge red crosses on the doors and on the roof. What could go wrong? In those days, even rebels respected the international sign. Of course nowadays, first responders are more likely targeted, and humanitarian workers are singled out for kidnapping and ransom in areas where the rule of law has disintegrated. But back then I wasn't worried about being a target. I worried about what state the nine-month-old was in. It was now more than forty-eight hours since he had been shot.

"Amare, do you know Debre Zeit? Can you find where they live?" I asked.

"I got good directions," he responded.

This was my first trip to this city. Normally it takes around three hours to get there. We were not driving fast, but there were no vehicles on the road. Amare drove into the city at around nine forty-five and found the house right away. John Williams, the father, was waiting at the gate and jumped up when he saw the ambulance. The compound gates were thrown open, and we pulled in. He was at the ambulance, pulling the door open.

"You are a sight for sore eyes," he said.

At the sound of the vehicle, his wife, Patricia, came running to the front door. I jumped out of the ambulance and went around to the back door. I pulled out the first aid supply bags that Mike had packed.

"Take me to your son," I said.

He was lying naked in his crib on his back, not moving. His eyes were closed.

"He stopped taking liquids last night," Patricia said.

Baby John was panting with his mouth open, and his lips were dry and crusted. I pinched the skin on his abdomen, which stood up like a tent and did not retract with the normal elasticity. He was extremely dehydrated.

"So where was he shot?" I asked.

Patricia pointed to the left lower abdomen, where I saw a puncture wound about the circumference of a number 2 yellow pencil.

"That's not the problem," she said. "Look at his back."

As I turned John Jr. on his side, he gave a high-pitched moan. "Oh my God," I muttered.

A deep, open, fleshy wound about three inches in circumference oozed blood and plasma. The bandage that had covered it was now sticking to the bed sheet. While the entry wound to the abdomen was small and discrete, the exit path had made a huge, gaping wound. The musculature that normally covered the back and the kidney was all mangled up. It was such a mess I couldn't distinguish muscle from kidney. The bullet had made a mess of the soft structures. I laid him back, supine.

"I need to get an IV in quick, and then I can clean the wound," I said.

I threw the first aid kit up on the single bed and started pulling out supplies, seeing what was there. I quickly put up the mobile IV pole and hooked up the catheters to intravenous solution. And I had my choice of myriad sizes of butterfly needles. When I was a pediatric resident, I could place these needles in the smallest scalp vein with my eyes closed. But it was fifteen years since I had done clinical hospital work. And baby John was severely dehydrated. I couldn't find any veins. The boy had seemed semi-comatose when I first walked into the room, but with the first prick of the needle searching for a vein, he came back swinging his arms. He was a fighter. His mom could barely hold the upper body still.

"Call your husband in," I said. "I can't have the kid moving."

Some forty minutes later and botched attempts on the feet, the ankles, both wrists, and the backs of the hands, I *finally* managed to get the IV slowly dripping. Sweat was pouring down my face, and my T-shirt was drenched. I mixed up antibiotics and injected them into the baby's thigh.

"I'm going to have to clean the wound," I said.

Patricia rushed from the room crying. "I can't stand to look at it!"

John, the father, nodded and said, "What do you want me to do?"

"Stabilize the arm, and don't let the IV be pulled out." I folded sterile drapes and put little John on his side again. He started to holler again but then fainted from the pain. I needed more light and picked up a flashlight. The flesh looked raw and hot, but I didn't see any pus forming. I pulled on sterile gloves. I took a syringe with sterile water and flushed the wound thoroughly three times. I covered the wound with sterile bandages that supposedly would not stick to the skin. I went outside and asked Amare to bring in the stretcher. He could help me transfer the kid to the stretcher, and we could tape down the arm so the IV would be secure. Before moving the stretcher to the ambulance, I gave baby John some Valium. I wanted him to sleep all the way to Addis.

I glanced at my watch. It was almost half past noon.

I told Mr. Williams, "Go get the things you want to take to Addis. We're leaving in fifteen minutes."

I repacked the medical supplies in the equipment bag and took them out to the ambulance. Then Amare and I rolled the stretcher to the ambulance. The child was sleeping peacefully. I just wanted to head back to Addis. Everyone climbed in, and Amare checked all the doors to make sure they were secure and locked. I pulled out my two-way radio.

"Tango One, Tango One, this is Whiskey. Come in. Over."

"Whiskey, Whiskey, go ahead. Over."

"We are loaded up and ready to return. Over."

"Negative, negative. This is Tango One. Embassy is being attacked. Stay where you are. Over."

"Roger. Wilco. Over."

"Tango One, over and out."

Jesus. I turned to John and Patricia in the back of the ambulance. We were stunned and devastated. The embassy, which was our safe haven, was being attacked? I couldn't process the event. Why was the US Embassy being attacked and by whom? I was momentarily speechless. I didn't have a plan for this occurrence. Now what to do? John was holding his wife in his arms, and she was sobbing uncontrollably. God, I did not want to stay here! I had no nursing assistant and, to be honest, the care the child needed was not going to be found in Addis either.

I turned to them and said, "Look, the best chance for your child is to reach Addis and for the embassy to call the Flying Doctors of Kenya to come evacuate you. Staying here gets us nowhere. But we can't go to the embassy."

I looked at John Williams and asked, "Does ILRI have a medical unit on the main campus? Do they have nurses always manning the unit?"

"Yes, it's only a two-bed unit, but the nurses are good. If you leave the supplies, they could take care of us."

"Amare, can you take us on back roads to the ILRI in Addis? I don't know what's going on, but it's clear we cannot enter on the main roads. We need to skirt the city and go directly to the research center," I said.

"I think I know a way," he said deliberately.

"We all have to agree on this. The embassy was clear that we should stay put. So, let's vote."

No one wanted to stay. Next, I asked what passports everyone carried. Patricia was American, but she had both American and British passports. She needed to hide her US passport and have both of their UK passports ready and available. I had my UN laissez-passer ID that didn't specify nationality, but my accent would give me away. We discussed how I would pretend to be Ethiopian and let Amare, the driver, talk for me. Ethiopian women could appear somewhat passive and subservient at times. If soldiers stopped us, our story was that we were going to ILRI.

I turned off the two-way radio and hid it under my seat. I looked at Amare.

"Let's go!" I said.

The road leaving Debre Zeit now had a few vehicles on it. They looked like farmer cooperative small trucks with produce inside, heading for a local market. Once Amare angled off on a side dirt track, we didn't run into another motor vehicle. This trail was deserted. We passed small villages and the people scampered out from their *tulkuls* (grass and mud huts) to stare at us, but we didn't slow down to talk. It was almost five in the afternoon by the time we finally pulled up to the gates of ILRI. John Williams stuck his head out and greeted the guard, who recognized him immediately. He swung open the gates, and John directed us to the health unit. He ran in to alert the staff. What a welcome sight.

Amare rolled the stretcher into the emergency room. Baby John was still sleeping. He also had peed a dark yellow patch on the diaper that lightly covered him. I looked at him and thought, I have no idea how that bullet entered you, but you are one lucky bug. It appeared not to have hit any major organ like the kidney, or at least one was still functioning. And he wasn't septic from the bullet nicking the intestines. It was time for another shot of antibiotics. I took out all the supplies and laid them on the counter. I turned to the two nurses.

"Let's try and keep the IV open and rehydrate him well."

I listened to his abdomen, and he had faint bowel sounds. This was a good sign. The X-ray from Debre Zeit was of poor quality, and grainy. You could clearly see a bullet lodged next to the L4 (lumbar) vertebra, and baby John was not moving his legs.

"Is your landline working?" I asked one of the nurses.

"Yes, it's in the next room," she indicated.

I pulled out my little book of telephone numbers and dialed the embassy's consular line.

"Hello, Mike, this is Connie. We're at ILRI!" I said.

"We tried to get you on the radio again, but you had turned it off," Mike replied gravely.

And then I told him the child was doing OK, but he needed to be evacuated ASAP. The nurses at ILRI could look after him, and if the ambulance was available, it could pick me up in the morning to bring me to check on him and to change bandages. But his best hope was to get to Nairobi!

Mike gave me an abbreviated synopsis of the events of the day—which, even after I heard it from the horses' mouth, still sounded totally bizarre. A false rumor had gone around the city that the Americans had invited the Tigrayans to enter the city. A mob had headed up to protest in front of the US Embassy. The city was now under the control of the Tigrayan rebels and everything was relatively quiet. A mandatory curfew lasted from seven in the evening to seven in the morning, and anyone out on the streets would be shot! So we needed to get moving and have Amare drop me at my house.

As I headed for the exit, I looked into the ER and the parents were huddled over the baby. They looked up and smiled and whispered a *thank you*.

"I'll be back in the morning. Try and get some rest," I said.

It was strange being back in Addis. A few people hurried through the streets, heading home with groceries in their hands. We avoided the central part of Addis where the Palace was located, so I had no idea as to the extent of the damage to the Palace or how many government forces died defending the capital. The light was fading fast, and Amare needed to go all the way across town to get to the embassy. I jumped out of the ambulance with the radio in my hand, as the gates to my compound swung open.

"See you tomorrow morning, Amare. Thanks for everything."

I walked up the steps to the front door. My hand was shaking trying to fit the key in the lock. Only now I realized that I had not eaten all day and how nerve-racking the whole experience was. I switched on all the lights in the living room and asked the guard to make a fire. I needed to wind down. I opened the fridge door and saw I had eggs and cheese. I was starving! An omelet was fast and would do the trick. As I settled down on the sofa before the fireplace with a cold St. George beer in my hand, the telephone rang. I hoped nothing was wrong with the baby.

It was the embassy!

"Connie, I want to thank you for going to the aid of the Williams family. They were so relieved to be back in Addis. We're working, as we speak, to get the Flying Doctors here. I know money can't approach repaying you for what you did today, but the embassy would like to reward your—"

"Mike, you can't *pay* me! I work for the UN," I said.

A meaningful pause extended, and then I continued, "But one day, I'm going to ask you for a favor."

"Wait, Connie, what do you mean?"

I shrugged my shoulders and said, "I don't know. But you owe me one!"

Chapter 24

The Flying Doctors

Amare, in the ambulance, was at the house early on May 30, and we headed to ILRI. Baby John was taking fluids by mouth, so the IV was removed. No word yet from the embassy about when the Flying Doctors might arrive. I had just finished cleaning the back wound at the ER, when I got the call on the landline.

"That was the embassy," I stated. "The rebel government has agreed to open the airport for two hours tomorrow morning, May 31, for the Flying Doctors. We must be at the airport at exactly 8 a.m."

The ambulance rolled up to the airport ahead of time. I jumped out on the tarmac and looked around. We heard the buzz of a small plane before we saw it. Then another ambulance unexpectedly drew up on the tarmac. Another UN staff member was also being evacuated. The single-propeller aircraft taxied up to where we were stationed. The pilot-doctor jumped out of the plane and said, "Let's get moving."

We put baby John in first on the stretcher, in an area cleared out to hold it. The UN staff person climbed gingerly in next. I said goodbye to the parents, and John Williams climbed in next.

I grabbed Patricia's hand, slipped my business card in her palm, and folded her fingers around it.

"When everything is known, probably in eight to nine months, can you write to let me know how everything turned out for the baby?" I asked.

She nodded, hugged me and jumped into the plane.

The pilot slammed the side door shut. He looked at me and said, "There's one more seat by the pilot. Do you want to come?"

Did I want to get on that plane? You betcha! But intuition told me to stay.

I shook my head, no. I waved them off and climbed slowly back in the ambulance. It was Saturday. I could go back home.

I fell into a deep sleep, which I sorely needed. When I finally woke up, it was already another day—June 1. I reached for the phone to call Monica.

"I was wondering when I'd finally hear from you," Monica said.

"Sorry it's taken me so long. But the last few days have been hairy."

And I proceeded to tell her about Debre Zeit and eventually putting the Williams family on the plane. Then I asked her why the US Embassy was attacked.

"Explain this to me as if I were a fifth grader!"

It seemed people in the capital thought the US "invited" the Tigrayan rebels to enter the city, when the reality was that the embassy was hoping the peace talks could start in London on Monday. At the time, the other Western embassies and nongovernmental agencies hoped an agreement among all parties could be reached about entry into the capital. Sometimes, however, life overtakes wishful thinking. Those rebels fighting on the ground were too close to victory to stop.

The provisional government imposed a curfew. It was enforced. But UN folks were feeling stir-crazy. Normally, my little group of close friends would meet for brunch every Sunday at the Hilton. The plan was to continue that tradition. I wanted desperately to "debrief" with my friends and get some much-needed emotional support.

"I'll be at the Hilton at eleven," I said.

I needed a good meal! The last few days had been rough, and my diet had been hit and miss.

No daytime curfew existed. Even so, traffic on the road was noticeably less. I'm sure the population in the capital was taking a wait-and-see approach to the newly arrived army. It was probably best to stay put at home. I suppose my colleagues were looking for some semblance of return to normalcy. This was what we did on Sundays. I was driving the loaner car from the office with UN plates. I expected no problem. On pulling into the Hilton parking lot, I was met by an armed soldier with rifle drawn.

I slowed down and stopped. He indicated for me to get out of the car. He had the gun, so I complied. As I faced him, I realized that he was just a boy. He couldn't be more than fourteen years old! He was skinny, and his uniform was worn and dirty as if he had marched the last 250 miles into the city. He probably did! He had a huge Afro. He looked nervous. Now I was nervous that a teenage boy had a rifle loosely aimed in my direction. I looked intently at him, trying to discern what he wanted me to do. I was wearing jeans, and my red bandana was covering my head.

He walked past me and tried to open the back passenger door. It was locked. Ditto for the trunk.

"I can open the trunk if you want," I offered.

And, with hands out in front of me, I walked slowly and deliberately to the driver's door to reach in and pop open the trunk. He looked into a mainly empty trunk with a spare tire. Then he slammed it closed. He motioned me back in the car, and he stepped back a few inches and lowered the rifle. I took that to mean I could go in and park the car. I made a conscious decision to not make any hurried movement and to slowly drive off. I parked quickly and hurried into the hotel. Another soldier was at the entry, looking over all who entered. However, he did not search my purse. I headed for the restaurant. Monica was already there, with a table for eight.

We hugged and collapsed in the chairs. It was good to see friends again and to hear what they had experienced when the Tigrayan army rolled into town. None of my friends lived close to the Palace, where most of the heavy fighting occurred. We remarked that there had been no reports of entry into houses or looting of valuables. This was remarkable when you review typical war reports of destruction and pillage. Only later did we learn that the entering troops had been given explicit directives not to enter houses; they were not to plunder anything! They were not to ask for even a glass of water! If anyone disobeyed, their own immediate army supervisor was to shoot him or her dead! As far as I could see, the directives were extremely effective. Tensions had been extremely high in the capital, waiting for the rebels to enter. The demeanor of the rebel army effectively defused a volatile situation. We were all looking forward to getting back on Monday to our respective offices and getting to work. At least, that was the scenario we wanted to happen.

Chapter 25

House on Fire

Monday, June 3, was hectic at the office. All the national staff reported in, and fortunately none had been affected by any of the fierce fighting. The WHO/EPR Centre still had expatriate staff to evacuate. The Suleiman family was sheltering in the Hilton. In addition, Dr. Roma was not able to get on a flight to Nairobi before the government shut down the airport. I knew UNDP (the United Nations Development Programme) was working with the provisional government to open the airport, so the rest of the UN nonessential staff could depart. I needed to update Geneva by email on what had occurred during the Tigrayan army take over. I was called for periodic updates with other UN Heads on the evolving situation in the capital. The new provisional government composed of two rebel groups (Tigray People's Liberation Front, and Eritrean People's Liberation Front) had joined forces and now called themselves the Ethiopian People's Revolutionary Democratic Front. They were intent on finding and imprisoning officers from Mengistu's army. The soldiers from Mengistu's army, if they had not already surrendered, were therefore trying to blend in with the population and make it back to their home districts and families.

People said you could get a Kalashnikov cheap for only 50 USD in the Mercado. It made sense. The soldiers would be ditching their army uniforms and rifles and anxious to find peasant clothing. I didn't need a rifle, but I did ponder over who was interested in buying those arms.

I was exhausted by the end of the day and headed home to the house off the Debre Zeit Road. I made a quick dinner and sat in front of a roaring fire in the living room and tried to decompress. As I headed for bed, the coals in the fireplace were still glowing hot. I figured I would leave the coals to go out on their own, as the morning fire would be easier to get started. Besides, the fireplace had a screen in front. What could go wrong? I closed the wooden shutters on the windows in the living room, crawled into bed, and immediately dropped off into a deep sleep. Somewhere in the distance I could hear faint, sporadic gunshots, which were starting to be a nightly lullaby for me.

I awoke suddenly to an intense orange-yellow light that lit up my bedroom but seemed to be coming from the living room. I jumped out of bed, hoping against hope that a fire had not started inadvertently in the living room. The fire screen was in place and no embers glowed. But the strange light was coming through the kitchen windows that faced northeast. I raced to the kitchen and beheld a huge blazing ball of fire shoot up into the sky at least forty feet. Oh my God, what was this? I glanced at my wristwatch, and it said 4:50 a.m. I couldn't calculate how far away I was from the blaze, but my first thought was that I was going to be burned to death if this spread. My second thought was to call Monica. She lived in a neighborhood at a higher elevation. She should be able to see something.

"Monica, sorry to wake you at this hour," I said. "But there is a huge fireball lighting up the sky in my neighborhood! If this catches on, I'm going to burn to death."

"Jesus, Davis, calm down. Let me go to my living room." After a few seconds she came back to the landline. "I don't see anything, but my living room doesn't face your area directly."

"Well, I'm in a really hard place. If I leave the house, I could be shot because the curfew is still in place. If I stay, this whole neighborhood is likely to go up in smoke."

"I'll get UN Security on the phone and get back to you," Monica said as she slammed down the phone.

I rushed to get on some clothes and to find my purse, which held my passport, driver's license, and UN laissez-passer. As I rushed again to the kitchen windows, I noticed the small, worn, leather messenger-type bag that sat forlornly in the foyer. The UN had issued explicit directives to essential staff. In case of emergency evacuation, we could bring only one small bag with us. No exceptions. The bag needed to be packed and ready to go *yesterday*.

I had a bad feeling in my gut, telling me to get out of the house. So I went out of the front door and headed out into the vast garden. I was about six feet from the house and I glanced back, still able to see the fireball which seemed even larger than before. Suddenly, a *huge mushroom cloud* appeared in the sky, engulfing the fireball. What the hell! I couldn't believe the Ethiopian government had nuclear weapons! In the space of a second, the air around me was under a vast sucking sensation that I fought against, pulling me towards the cloud vortex. In that instant, I realized how idiotic it was to be looking directly at this. As I turned to run in the opposite direction, away from the turbulence, a huge roar and shock wave erupted, later said to measure 6.9 on the Richter scale. The force of the shock wave from the blast blew out all the shuttered windows and the roof of the house, and it hurled me to the ground. Then I heard the sound of rockets going off, and I saw shards of shrapnel plummeting to the ground in my neighbor's compound.

As I slowly picked myself up from the ground, Ferkete and the family guard rushed around from the back of the house. She stared at me and was about to say something, when the sound of more rockets peppered the air. We speedily sought refuge under the extended eaves of the house, which surrounded the entire front of the building. I sank down on the grass and braced my back against the house siding. The rocket explosions intensified. The guard was kneeling and prostrating himself, bowing down to the ground, murmuring Coptic prayers. Ferkete was crying. I was desperately trying to make an escape plan! I had lived in the house for less than three weeks. Due to the curfew, it was probably wise to avoid a main road exit. But I had no idea of the surrounding neighborhood or where the warren of tiny service roads led. When the din from the exploding rockets quieted, I quickly asked Ferkete some questions.

"If we turn right after exiting, where does that road take us?" I asked.

She just stared at me.

"Is the service road big enough for my car to get through?"

She did not comprehend any of my words. I shook her upper arm.

"Ferkete, you've got to focus and help us get out of here!"

Finally, she said, "I don't know where the road leads."

And then the rockets and rain of shrapnel started again. Well, if I had to walk out of there, I had better get my purse and the evacuation bag from the foyer. I know you're not to go back into a burning building, but I needed some identification. The front door had slammed and locked from the inside, but the living room's immense plate glass windows from ceiling to floor were completely blown out. So I walked through the windows. I grabbed my purse and the messenger bag and retreated the same way I had entered. Interestingly, the UN poster warning the rebels not to enter a diplomatic compound was still attached to the door.

Now, what was the safer option for me? Should I carry this bag through the chaotic streets? It actually contained all my antique silver neck crosses, necklaces, and bracelets collected over the last nine months. If stopped by roaming vandals, I would lose everything. I made an instant decision. I would hide the bag in the huge garden with copious thick shrubs and trees. If looting occurred—and normally there was looting after any kind of disaster—if thugs broke into the house, they wouldn't find anything of value. I do not recommend hiding a suitcase in a garden, in the midst of rockets exploding overhead, but I did it anyway.

So this was my plan. Wait for a lull in the shelling. Listen for other compound gates opening. Blend in with the crowd leaving these homes. Stay with the crowd for safety until I see a familiar road. Then make it back to the UN compound at the ECA building. The UN Security Team had created an office on the top floor of one of the two twin towers, which were nine stories high. They had good reception for the shortwave radio setup and could see what was happening in the city. If I could just make it to the UN compound, I would be safe. I glanced at my watch. It was a little after seven. It's funny how I got used to the sound of rockets firing. I could almost curl up in a ball and try to fall off to sleep. Until the sounds of shelling stopped. It was the silence that stirred me. I heard nearby gates opening, and the guard and I rushed to our gate and cautiously opened it. A roaring stream of what looked like refugees with suitcases and small children sitting on the shoulders of their fathers flowed past. It looked like a scene out of a documentary. Then I heard the hum of a car drawing out of a compound. So a car could go that way!

"Ferkete, cars are leaving, so I'm taking the office vehicle. I'll drop you and the guard off at the first major road, unless you want to go towards the UN," I said.

Ferkete ran to get a few things from her room and I grabbed my purse. We jumped into the car. The guard opened the gate cautiously and I drove the car into the lane. I waited for the guard to lock the gate from the inside and to climb over the wall. Then he climbed in the back seat of the car, and we were off. We were silent. The car could only creep slowly along because of the mass of people in the small lane. I didn't recognize any landmarks. It took about thirty minutes to get to a big road. Ferkete told me to pull over to the side of the road. The guard hopped out.

"I'm getting off here. My cousins live out this way," she said. Then she pointed in the opposite direction. "If you go back the other way, you'll eventually come out near Lenin Square and will know where you are. We'll be in touch. Good luck," she said and hopped out of the car.

I felt confident. And although I still didn't recognize anything on this side of Addis, I was in a UN-plated car and I had ID. Just keep on driving. Scarily, it looked to me like most people were going in the exact opposite direction to where I was headed. That made me nervous. Finally, I saw the ECA conglomeration of buildings on the hill! I knew where I was now, and quickly maneuvered to the employee entrance. Great, I recognized the guard on duty and rolled down the window.

"Dr. Davis, are you all right?" he asked. His voice sounded far off in the distance.

He sounded concerned. It was only then that I looked down at my shirt. It was torn and in tatters, and my arms were showing through the long sleeves. How did that happen, I wondered?

"Yeah, I'm fine. I live near the explosion. Is UN Security still in the towers?"

"Yes, but the explosion cut power. No elevator! You'll have to walk up to the roof!"

I nodded and drove up to parking spaces close to the towers. As I exited the car, I noticed the hanging walkway between the two towers dangling and swinging in the wind. It had to be some force to tear that off! I walked to the farthest tower. Most of the windows on the lower floors of the tower were blown out. I took a deep breath, opened the door, and started to climb. I was not looking forward to this. I had to rest for ten minutes on the fifth-floor landing and then again on the seventh floor, before I finally reached the top floor. As I struggled through the open doorway on the ninth floor, breathing heavily, I heard.

"Whiskey, Whiskey, this is Tango One. Do you read me? Over."

I answered with a catch in my throat. "I read you loud and clear. Over!"

Chapter 26

Supplies Needed

All three radio officers turned in their chairs to stare at the phantom.

"Connie, we thought you were dead!" they cried in unison.

"I thought I was, too," I said.

Then Mark, the most senior officer, picked up a landline and said to no one in particular, "I better call Monica. She's been calling every five minutes to find out if we've heard from you."

I sank into a chair. I overheard his conversation telling Monica that, once the UN heard from the government that the explosion was under control, she could come to the UN to pick me up. They were still looking at me strangely. Only later did Monica tell me my hair was in disarray and I was covered in ashes. I explained that the shock wave from the explosion had blown out the roof and all the windows at the house I was renting. It was going to be unlivable for some time.

"Are there any other UN folks who live out my way?" I asked.

They weren't sure and sent someone to go look up addresses. And then the landline started ringing again. I could hear a one-sided conversation as John, another of the radio operators, was taking down notes.

It seemed the Dejazmach Balcha Memorial Hospital, supported by the Russians, had run out of supplies—particularly surgical supplies. They needed a UN doctor to come over to assist in surgery. They had a badly wounded foreigner.

"The Russian Hospital has been requesting the UN doctor to come out of his house in preparation for any casualties," John told me. "But he's having some sort of mental breakdown and refuses to budge."

"Get the doctor on the landline," I said.

He dialed and handed me the phone. I turned my back towards the radio operators and cupped my hand around the mouthpiece.

"Hello, this is Dr. Davis. I've just come from the Debre Zeit Road area where my house was demolished by the explosion. I physically am unable to offer assistance to anyone due to my present condition. But you were not involved in the explosion. The hospitals are calling for supplies and medical assistance in surgeries. The UN is sending the ambulance to collect you right now. I will go down to the supply room and put together emergency supplies for the hospital. We don't know if any more UN staff will be arriving hurt. *We need you here.*" I glanced towards the staff and whispered into the phone receiver. "If you do not come right now, let me warn you: I will report this to the highest level concerned. You will never work for the UN ever again. We need you, stat!" I slammed down the phone.

"Please don't tell me the supply unit is on the ground floor," I said to the radio operators.

"No, it's in the basement." Mark laughed.

I wasn't up to walking down those flights of stairs again. But it had to be done. Once in the basement, I threw supplies into two large cartons. I wondered how many wounded would come in from the explosion. They would have horrific burn wounds.

By the time I got the medical supplies ready, Monica had arrived. Fortunately, the Security Team sent a chauffeur down to find me and collect the medical supplies to be transported. No way could I hike back up all those flights of stairs to say goodbye to the radio operators.

"They called me to come pick you up," Monica said. I could see her lips were moving but I was having trouble understanding her.

She was standing right in front of me but sounded like she was underwater, and I could barely hear her.

"I think I have hearing damage. I can hardly hear you. You sound a million miles away and underwater," I said as I rubbed my ears.

I followed her to the car.

"Tell me everything!" she said.

And I proceeded to outline what had happened since our last telephone call. I looked around for my purse and checked my IDs. Crap, it seemed I had left my radio in my briefcase in the living room of the Debre Zeit (DZ) house. My clothes were also over there. The evacuation messenger bag with the silver jewelry was hidden in the garden. Monica assured me it would be safe. The interim government had announced that no one was to try and reenter the area presently, or they would be shot. They would announce on national radio when residents could go back to retrieve items. The only thing to do was to go relax at Monica's apartment. Thank God, I didn't have to climb any stairs. Her elevator worked, and their building was intact. Yet, I found it difficult to relax.

Monica's apartment, on the fifth floor of the building, had an expanse of windows along the entire length of the living room. I hated that feeling of "openness." She had no curtains or blinds, because she didn't need them at that height. But I felt exposed somehow. Sporadic gunfire could still be heard throughout the city. It made me jumpy.

"Connie, come sit down over here at the kitchen table."

But her voice sounded like it was in a tunnel and she was at the far end. I sat down as far away from the windows as possible. She placed a sandwich before me. I wasn't particularly hungry. I stared off into space. I heard the rat-a-tat-tat of gunfire again and I flashed back to the orange-red glow of the fireball in my living room. I rubbed my arms. I felt a fine pebbly substance just below the skin level that went the length of both arms. I wasn't bleeding, but I wanted to scrape the granules out of my skin. But whatever it was, it was embedded.

"Connie, why don't you go to the bathroom and brush your hair, wash your face. Even better, take a shower," Monica encouraged.

I slowly moved to the bathroom and turned on the light. This stranger gazed back from the mirror. I removed the rubber band from my ponytail and started to slowly brush out the tangles. Fine-grained particles of rocks and dirt and shiny crystals of silicon and glass filtered down. This must be the remains of the shattered windows ground down into fine particles. That must be what was just below the surface on my forearms. I dropped my clothes and stepped into a hot shower. I was sore from having been blown to the ground by the force of the explosion. I realized I was lucky to be alive. If the house were three blocks closer to the epicenter, I suspected I wouldn't have been looking into that mirror right then. I stood in the hot shower until I couldn't stand up any longer. As I exited the shower, I glanced once again in the mirror.

"Monica!" I shouted. And I rushed out to the living room with the towel wrapped around me. "My eyebrows have turned white, completely white!" I screamed.

"I think you need to rest," she said.

I'd heard about this kind of thing happening if someone had a big stress, but I thought it was a myth. Maybe I just needed some sleep.

I went and put on one of Monica's T-shirts that she had thoughtfully laid out, then wandered back into the living room. Monica looked up.

"You know the foreigner the hospital called about, for you to send medical supplies?" Monica asked. "You won't believe who that is."

"Who?"

"Remember the Kenyan photographer who exposed the Ethiopian famine back in the 80s, Mohamed Amin? He was in town and happened to be filming the fireball with his soundman when the explosion occurred. His soundman was killed, and they operated on Amin. They had to amputate his left arm!"

"Oh my God! He was in the wrong place, at the wrong time, this time around," I muttered.

"UN Security called. They said the interim government would open your neighborhood tomorrow from ten to noon for residents to retrieve needed items. The UN will send a driver tomorrow so you can go back to collect your things."

"Monica, thanks for letting me stay here, but I think I'll move to the Hilton tomorrow. It'll take more than a month to repair damage to the house! I don't want to be a burden."

"Connie, you don't have to leave yet. In fact, I think you should stay with somebody," she said knowingly.

It had grown dark and the streetlights were lit. Monica had all the lights on in the apartment, and I felt we stood out among the other darkened apartments. You could hear the rumble of a tank in the distance and the sound of gunfire again. I rushed over to the light switch on the wall and quickly extinguished the lights.

"It's not safe sitting here exposed, where everyone can see us. We're sitting ducks if they want to train their rifles on us," I said.

Monica stared at me. I looked around the room and noted the distance from the plate glass windows and where the entry door was located. I chose a stuffed sofa chair close to the kitchen table, and I sank down on the floor using the side of the chair to support my back. Monica was about to say something, and then thought better of it.

"Fine, Connie, we can sit on the floor if you want. Let me go turn off the lights in the bedrooms."

After about ten minutes she returned with a fourteen-inch-tall beeswax candle, about four inches in diameter. She then went into the kitchen, opening up cabinets and drawers and slamming cabinet doors around.

"What are you doing, Monica?"

She came back into the living room with her arms filled with supplies. She had matches, a big bag of marshmallows, chocolate Hershey bars, graham crackers and some St. George beer.

"If we're going to sit on the floor, let's have a campfire!"

And she proceeded to spread a bedspread on the floor, partially under the dining room table. Then she lit the candle, which gave a soft, calm, amber glow to the room. And then she opened the marshmallows.

"Where did you find these?" I asked.

Turns out, a departing American family had gifted these items to her before they were evacuated two months earlier! I had to laugh. I slipped a marshmallow on a fork and slowly turned it in the single-wick flame of an Ethiopian candle. Just concentrating on keeping the marshmallow from going up in flames was a welcome relief from worrying about my messenger bag hidden somewhere in Ferkete's garden. I slipped my golden-brown, soft, gooey marshmallow onto the graham cracker. I topped it with a Hersey's square and another cracker. This former Girl Scout counselor at Flying G Ranch Girl Scout Camp, knew a thing or two about roasting marshmallows. I don't know what we talked about. Maybe we didn't talk. But that night I slept like a baby for the first time in days, with no thoughts of exploding rockets.

Chapter 27

Back to Hilton

I opened my eyes to the light in the room once again, but it was the regular light of morning breaking. It took a minute to remember where I was. I rubbed my ears, but normal sound was still elusive. I didn't want to get up, but I needed to find out about the national staff of the EPR Centre and how soon the UN could convince the provisional government to open the airport so they could evacuate the remaining expat staff. Certainly, the UN rep would be calling a meeting. We still needed to get out nonessential staff members to Nairobi. I sure hoped Dr. Roma had not experienced any problems. I wondered when we would hear anything further about who and what had caused the explosions. How many people had died? Would we ever really know? I could hear Monica faintly in the kitchen.

By the time I got to the kitchen, Monica was almost ready to leave for work.

"You could have slept in a little longer," she said. "Nobody is expecting you at work today."

"I need to get back into a routine," I said. "There'll be meetings, and I need to check that my national staff are all fine. After I collect my things from the DZ house, I'll head to the office. We probably have some broken windows there."

"Call me later and let me know if you decide to come back and stay here for a while," she said as she closed the apartment door.

I still felt like I was in a fog. I moved like I had been in a wreck. My eyebrows were still grey. Monica had left me coffee and toast. I was roused by the soft ping of the doorbell. It was the UN driver. An hour had passed, and I was still sitting in a kitchen chair, not sure what to tackle first. Well, it was decided for me. The curfew for the DZ area would be lifted for a short two hours. Best to get over there and be ready to go in. The police saw my UN plates and waved us though. That was helpful, because I had nothing to show I lived in the area. I directed the driver to the house. The gates were still shut. I asked the driver to climb over, because the guard had locked the deadbolt from the inside. We drove close to the wall, and he used the hood to get a purchase on the wall and was able to scale it rather easily. He flung open the gates and we drove the vehicle in and closed the entryway.

Jesus, it wasn't a dream. It looked like a disaster! The roof was sunken in. All the windows were blown out, including the shutters that closed them from the outside. Then I raced to the far side of the garden and looked under a bottlebrush bush. Yes, thank God, my messenger bag sat exactly where I had left it. I picked it up, checked the insides—which seemed untouched—and threw it in the car. Once again, I walked to the front of the house and through the front plate glass windows of the living room, now without even any shards hanging on. It was depressing. Dirt and wood from the ceiling covered the sofa and chairs. It was a good thing I was wearing closed toe shoes, because I was walking on a lot of glass and other rubbish. I went to the master bedroom and pulled my suitcase from the closet and placed it on the bed. I didn't have a lot of clothes, and I just wanted to hurry up and fold them and put them in the suitcase. I checked the bathroom and rapidly picked up the toothpaste and brush and some cosmetics.

I went into the guest bedroom. The roof here was hanging down lower, and more precariously, than in the master bedroom. I glanced around the room. The windows here faced the back service area. Miraculously, one was still intact. I had planned for this to be the nursery for the baby. I had even located a Western-style crib that was to be delivered in the following week. Now, a thin wooden rafter hung by a sliver from the roof. A layer of dust and dirt covered the entire room. I gave thanks I didn't have an infant with me. She might have been hurt in the explosion.

I walked into the kitchen and pulled a notebook out of my purse. I ripped a sheet out of the memo pad and scrawled hurriedly.

"Ferkete, so sorry about the state of the house, but at least no one was hurt." No words could describe the wreckage before my eyes. I wished her well and said we'd be in touch.

I had paid her for the month, so she had some funds for what looked like a lengthy repair. I took one last look around the living room and then grabbed the suitcase in the foyer with one hand and my brief case with the radio in it with the other hand, and slowly walked through the blown-out windows.

Chapter 28

Appeal

We left the same way we had arrived. The driver drove the SUV out through the gates of the compound. He once again locked the gates from the inside. After he scaled the wall, we headed for the Hilton Hotel. I needed a change of scenery and dreaded going back to the Ghion. It would be depressing to return to square one when I thought I was embarking on a new life. I talked to reception at the Hilton and told my account of living too close to the Debre Zeit explosion. I didn't know how long I needed to be in the hotel. I told them I didn't want to be high up on a floor because I felt exposed. The Hilton had basement rooms that didn't get a lot of light or noise. That suited me. They were also cheaper. So I registered and told them to expect me in the late afternoon. Then I was off to the office.

The EPR offices seemed to have escaped major damage. The national staff were back at the office. Everyone heard of my close call and crowded around to welcome me back with hugs. None of the EPR staff lived out my way, so they were all spared. Maryam said the government could not give an estimate of how many had been killed in the explosion.

The national newspaper said about ten thousand people lived in the shantytown surrounding the fuel depots for Mobil, Shell, and Total. The city's largest and heretofore secret ammunition depot was held in underground bunkers, near the fuel depots aboveground. Although never independently verified, it was reported that some disgruntled officers and soldiers from Mengistu's army, hoping to destabilize the new rebel provisional government, threw grenades at the fuel depots and into the munitions depot. Although the main fuel depots did not explode, the warehouse for liquid-gas canisters owned by the Italian Agip Corp. went up in the resulting inferno, creating a huge mushroom cloud and spraying the area with lethal shards of metal. The huge explosion erupted before dawn, rocking much of the city like a big earthquake and creating a firestorm of rockets, bullets, and shrapnel that ripped through the teeming slums surrounding it.

The Washington Post reported the following on June 5, 1991:

Many witnesses in the area reported hearing an exchange of automatic-weapons fire, then the glow of fire, before the explosion.

"I woke up to machine-gun firing around 4 a.m., but I thought, 'Well that's normal.' . . . Not much later a huge orange-red ball of fire seemed to fill my whole house. I thought my house was on fire . . . but it was the light from these huge balls of flame nearby," said Connie Davis, an American doctor with the World Health Organization, who lives several blocks away from the Agip warehouse.

Exploding munitions had shot out in all directions like deadly pinwheels, decapitating at least two people and igniting a chain reaction of other fires and explosions that continued throughout the day. The powerful concussive force of the blasts flattened a broad swath of houses around the depot, crumpled heavy metal shutters on shops, and blew out windows for miles around. The Washington Post reported more than 100 people killed and 130 wounded and said many more were believed buried beneath the rubble of their homes. Why would anyone in their right mind place an underground munitions depot close to large fuel depots in a packed urban area?

As I headed to my office, I checked on the status of the offices of the expat staff who had departed for Nairobi. Dr. Roma was in one of the offices.

"Connie, I'm so glad you weren't hurt in the explosion!" she said.

"Thanks," I said. "Where were you?"

Turns out her apartment was in another area of Addis that escaped the fighting. I told her I was waiting for a communication from UNDP to state when the airport would reopen and the rest of the UN staff could evacuate to Nairobi. I opened my office. Everything looked the same. I supposed the reason we had no windows blown out was because they didn't face the explosive force directly, but were turned parallel to it—on the side of the ECA building and not in the front. We were lucky! I sat down at my desk and stared off into the distance. My hearing still had not fully recovered and the tunnel effect was still there. And then the phone rang.

"Connie, this is WHO/Geneva. Are you all right?"

I think after the tenth time I retold the story, it started to have a cathartic effect. It provided a psychological release and a way to get some relief from the pent-up emotions. Geneva was calling to ask me to canvass the hospitals and to see what emergency supplies they needed. It would be good if I could write up and send them the emergency appeal within twenty-four hours. Well, that jolted me out of my stupor. I headed for Roma's office.

"Roma, I just got a call from Geneva. Can you help me canvass the major hospitals, to see what type of supplies they might need? I think you'll be leaving for Nairobi tomorrow, so we should each take a driver. Let's divvy up the list. We'll be back in two or three hours max!"

Once I realized that people were depending on the UN agencies to provide much-needed medical supplies, I could focus beyond my measly concerns. When we got back from the hospitals, I started writing up the appeal for donations—starting from the events of the takeover of the capital by the Tigrayan army. And then, seven days later, the explosion of the underground munitions depot rocked the capital. Particularly the latter episode had caused many hospitals and the Red Cross to use unprecedented numbers of supplies to treat the injured. Around four o'clock I got the call from UNDP. Roma was listed on the plane to leave tomorrow. I went down to her office, thanked her for her crucial assistance in gathering data for the appeal, and told her to head back to her apartment to repack and get ready for the car to take her to the airport tomorrow. Then I turned back to the computer to put the finishing touches on the appeal. I wanted to get it off to Geneva before the office day ended. I pushed the return button, and off it went.

I was exhausted, but it was a good kind of exhaustion. The canvassing had reset my epidemiologist's button and I was thinking like a disease detective once again. I returned to the Hilton basement garden room and ordered in. And then I fell into a deep sleep. I awoke refreshed, and it seemed like the fog I had been traveling in the last few days was partially lifted. My hearing was improving also! Maybe I wouldn't have serious repercussions from the explosion.

By the end of the week, my hearing had almost returned to normal. WHO/Geneva had sent out the appeal, and they were pleased the Centre had remained open. We still heard the occasional tank rumbling down the street at night. The Tigrayan and Eritrean rebels had won the war, but the Amhara population had not warmed up to the new provisional government. Sporadic skirmishes and gunfire continued. So armed patrols by the new provisional government and the curfew remained in effect. But what we all needed was a party! And Monica sent out invitations to the single UN essential staff that remained in the capital. The seven o'clock enforced curfew remained. That just meant we needed to start the party earlier. The invitation said: "Come for lunch and get home before seven. Bring your favorite drink to share." Once everyone had arrived, Monica brought in a sizable carton.

She opened it up and started distributing maroon army hats of the type seen on the rebel Tigrayan army soldiers. There was one for each of us!

"Where did you get these?" one of our friends asked.

"From the rebel army, duh," Monica said.

It seemed Monica had run into a sergeant in the rebel army and had negotiated a deal for twelve rebel army hats, in exchange for an unspecified number of condoms. I still have my maroon Tigrayan rebel army hat.

Chapter 29

Black Lion Hospital

It was Friday, June 14, and it was now nine days since the explosion of the underground munitions depot. All things considered, everything was going well. All the expat staff from the WHO/EPR Centre were now in Nairobi, since about one week earlier. Gun shots still made me flinch, and I noticed I didn't turn my back to any door when sitting. An ill-timed rocket could still trigger anxiety. But my hearing seemed almost back to normal! At the time I didn't know much about the condition termed post-traumatic stress disorder (PTSD).

I considered myself "jumpy," but otherwise normal enough to go back to work. I wanted to complete the meningitis manual, but now was not the time to convene meetings on that. I continued in the position of acting director and had plenty to do in that role. I usually got to the office early to have one hour to think, before other agencies started coming to me with their problems. And then the phone rang. This was fairly early for a call. I wondered who could be calling.

"Hello, Dr. Davis. This is Dr. Naviat at Black Lion Hospital. You need to come right away! There is a baby."

"A baby? What baby?" I said.

"Connie, I think you'll want to come to the pediatric ward. A female infant was brought into the orphan ward around five this morning. The nurses are calling her 'Konjit,' which means beautiful."

"I'll be right there." I quickly banged down the phone.

A baby. I wondered if she was found in the area of the explosion? Was she healthy? Best not to get my hopes up until I saw her. I went directly to Dr. Naviat's office. He had this huge grin on his face.

"I was on rounds this morning and the nurses were all talking about Konjit!" he said. "Let's go to the orphan ward."

Only one of the beds had an infant. I tiptoed over to the crib and peered in. She looked up at me with these incredible, immense, mahogany-colored, angel eyes. And I knew right then, in an instant!

I looked at Dr. Naviat and said, "This is the one. I can't believe it. This is the one."

And I reached in to pick up my daughter and placed her over my left shoulder. Dr. Naviat smiled and nodded and left me to get to know my infant daughter. She was beautiful and perfect, with ten fingers and toes. She looked about three or four months old. She didn't cry. She didn't smile. She just stared at me, wondering. Who is this person? I couldn't believe my luck that she looked so healthy. It was hard to put her down, but after about thirty minutes I placed her back in the crib and went to see Dr. Naviat.

"So, what do we know about her?"

"Go ask Genet in the emergency room. She's the social worker who went out to investigate."

I left immediately to go to Genet, who took me into one of the examination cubicles.

"I know why you're here. I worked the night shift, but I've been waiting for you," she said. And then she launched into the story. At about five thirty in the morning, two soldiers from the Tigrayan army marched into the ER with a baby in their arms. They were on patrol around St. George's Cathedral, as the curfew was still in force. They heard a baby crying and noticed an infant in a yellow handmade sweater and a thin blanket at the top of the steps in front of the huge cathedral doors. One of them picked her up, and she stopped crying. They looked around but could not spot anyone. Then they decided to bring her to Black Lion.

"I went out right away to the church to see if I could spot the mother. I think she wanted the *abuna*, the chief priest, to open the doors and find the child. She must be terribly upset that the soldiers found her instead. Now that it's after eight, I'll head to the surrounding neighborhoods to see if I can find out anything about a recently pregnant woman now without a child," Genet said.

"Thanks for all of your help," I said.

I headed out to the parking lot where the EPR driver waited for me. "Let's head back to the office."

Once there, I picked up the phone and called Monica.

"You are not going to believe this, but—"

"My spy Genet already called from Black Lion to say a baby had been found!"

"Hey, is there no privacy here?" I laughed. "Dr. Naviat called and said I better get over there because the nurses were calling this baby beautiful. And she is!"

"First things first. You better get her HIV tested. I'll go down to Debrework's office and get her to go over to the orphan ward." Monica hung up the phone.

"I'm not feeling well," I said to the secretaries. "I'm going to leave early. See you on Monday." I was hesitant to tell the secretaries about the infant, in case her blood tests turned out positive. I didn't want to get everyone excited and then discover a problem. I should be sure I could keep her.

Chapter 30

Waiting to Exhale

I couldn't do much until I heard from Debrework about the results of the HIV test. Every time I tried to review the meningitis manual, my mind started to wander. I tried to remember what Ethiopia's neonatal rate for HIV was. To keep busy and keep my mind off of things, I thought I would wash my underwear and hang it on the outside patio. Then I ordered room service, because I wanted to stay close to the phone. She called me in the early afternoon on Saturday, June 15.

"Connie, this is Debrework," she said. "I went over to Black Lion this morning to draw the blood. Your baby is so pretty. Now, I ran a quick and dirty test, and got a result. I can only do the definitive blood test on Monday because of my lab kits. I need to test ten infants at once, otherwise I waste nine tests. I won't share the results on your baby until I do the definitive test on Monday," she said.

Debrework hung up the phone before I could protest.

And the long wait began. I checked back in with Genet, and she described how she had gone back to two different neighborhoods that surrounded St. George's Cathedral, asking the community about recently pregnant women and whether they had their babies. She was unable to find out anything. The mother could have come from any neighborhood in the city. And because of the recent takeover of the capital and the disturbing explosion of the underground munitions, there had been a lot of movement and unsettlement in the city. Genet said she was making out her report—and would provide it to Dr. Naviat—that she was unable to find the mother or any relative and she had a cold case. She was reporting the infant as an orphan.

I contacted Dr. Naviat to find out the procedures for an orphan. They didn't like to keep the babies on the orphan ward for a long time. It only increased their odds of picking up some illness. So unless the orphan was sick and needed medical treatment, they usually called social services to start preparations to place the infant in an orphanage. Right now, the hospital didn't have adequate staff or formula for babies, and she was getting whole milk. The hospital could release the infant into the custody of an approved applicant, if they were adopting in Ethiopia. So *technically*, if the HIV/AIDS test was negative and the physical exam was normal, the hospital could release Konjit to me on Monday. I had a considerable amount of information to process.

This wasn't how I had imagined finding a baby. I was feeling a little overwhelmed by how fast things were progressing. I had wanted to have a comfortable apartment or house and to have a crib set up. I would already have friends looking for an ayah to help me with Konjit. Everyone would be excited and wanting to drop by to see the baby. But instead, I was waiting for the results of an HIV test before I could relax and be excited and happy. I needed to make a list of things to do. Maybe that would calm me. I should probably limit who came by at first, because I didn't want to introduce unwanted bugs and bacteria until I knew she was truly healthy. First thing in the morning, once I knew the

HIV result, I needed to call the US Embassy to get the doctor who did orphan exams to go over to Black Lion.

The Ministry of Labour and Social Welfare had given me permission to look for a child. I had passed the biggest hurdle. I found the infant I was looking for, so it was possible to take her out of the hospital on Monday if her tests were all negative. I needed to make a plan. When I got to the Hilton, I went to the reception. I explained that I needed a crib and a rocking chair placed in my basement room. I also inquired whether they had someone who could periodically "babysit" for a few hours a day. They did. I pulled out the baby clothes I bought in Nairobi. A red one-piece outfit (a snap-crotch bodysuit with feet) would be her coming-home outfit. A snap-crotch T-shirt would go underneath. I couldn't forget a diaper, and I put one in the bag. Oh yes, I already had a baby carrier. I put the diaper bag with assorted clothes and the baby carrier together on the couch. Everything was ready for the phone call.

Monday June 17

Debrework called me at around eleven on Monday.

"Good news, Connie," she said. "She's negative for HIV/AIDS and hepatitis."

"Great news! Let me call Dr. Naviat to start the ball rolling. I'll need a written lab report on the results. Thank you so much for coming in over the weekend to run the tests."

I then called Black Lion Hospital. "Dr. Naviat, good news. Konjit is negative for HIV/AIDS. I will be coming to pick her up. Can you do a physical exam and estimate her age, so we can determine birthdate? Once I'm there, I'll do my own exam. Oh, can you tell the nurses *not* to give a BCG shot, it will only complicate things later in the US?" And I hung up.

BCG, or bacille Calmette-Guerin, is a vaccine for tuberculosis (TB). BCG is used in many countries, like Ethiopia, with a high prevalence of TB, to prevent childhood tuberculous meningitis and miliary (disseminated) disease. However, BCG is not recommended for use in the United States because of the *low risk of infection with Mycobacterium tuberculosis, and the vaccine's potential interference with tuberculin skin test reactivity.* Since the tuberculin skin test is *routinely* used in the US to indicate whether you have been exposed to TB and whether you need TB treatment, having the BCG vaccination would only complicate our lives in the States!

I also called the Consulate Officer to get the name of the approved doctor to do the physical required by the embassy. He said he could send the doctor right over to the hospital that morning. I called for Abebayehu, my driver.

"I need to go to Black Lion Hospital," I said. "I've been approved to adopt and I'm picking up my baby today!"

Well, he was surprised but happy for me. I went straight to see Dr. Naviat. He confirmed that a doctor sent by the US Embassy had come earlier and examined the baby. He found her healthy and would write up a report and send it to the embassy.

My daughter was all eyes as I came to examine her. She had a strong heart, and I heard her cry, so I knew the lungs were strong. I checked her genitalia and saw she was intact, thank God. And then I checked her developmental milestones. Milestones are specific areas in motor coordination that most infants can do at three months, five months, etc. I estimated she was between three and three and a half months. I was anxious to see what Dr. Naviat thought. I was relieved that Konjit did not have any serious health problems and excited to be taking my infant home shortly.

"I think she's around three months. She is at the ninety-fifth percentile for height, and the forty-fifth percentile for weight," he said.

"OK, so she was born sometime in February." And Feb. 14, 1991 popped up in my mind. Valentine's Day. Great idea. Then the entire world will celebrate your birthday and Mom will never forget it!

Around this time, Monica arrived on the floor to take photos of the beaming mom. I was all thumbs taking out her new clothes, and putting the pale-yellow sweater, which looked hand-knit, to the side. The head nurse peeked in and asked if I could leave the clothes she arrived in for the orphan ward. They had so few items. And without thinking, I nodded, yes. It was only later, at the Hilton, that I wished I had kept them. One day, my daughter would ask if I had anything from those early days. It would have been a nice keepsake from her birth mother. But I gave it away. It was for a good cause I would say. And it was, but I still regret doing it. Monica got photos of the nurses on the orphan and pediatric wards. Everyone was excited for little Konjit. I went one last time into Dr. Naviat's office to thank him for calling me four days earlier.

He smiled and said, "Now remember, if you take her out today, you can't bring her back in a week or a month if you find out she has a congenital heart problem or anything. There are no returns. So, are you sure, Dr. Davis?"

I smiled and nodded. "But, Dr. Naviat, someone vaccinated her with BCG!" I said.

"You know, Connie, it's written hospital policy that all infants leaving must be checked and given BCG before leaving. They had already vaccinated her by the time I went in to tell them not to do it."

I would come to regret that policy when my daughter was starting school. We had difficulties when her tuberculin test showed positive, but what's done was done. And Monica and I headed to the elevators with my new baby in the baby sling. I was exhausted already, and I just wanted to get back to the hotel to collapse.

"Are you going to be OK with the baby?" Monica asked. "Do you need anything?"

"Hey, I'm a pediatrician," I said proudly. What could go wrong?

And I carefully got into the car. We hurried to the Hilton, and I headed immediately to my room. The Hilton had thoughtfully brought down one Bunsen burner and a sauce pan, so I could heat up the bottle with the formula. Thank goodness I bought the formula in Nairobi and made sure to pick it up when I gathered things from my bombed-out house in Debre Zeit. The stores and markets were still mostly closed. There had been looting after the underground explosion, and most small shop owners were staying closed until they got a better sense of which way events would go. It takes time for people to start trusting the intentions of the provisional government. No one knew if there would be continuing destabilizing events such as the munitions depot explosion. No one knew if other soldiers of the former regime still lurked around the city and could make things uncomfortable for the new provisional government.

Konjit started to get restless and began to cry. I tested the formula on the back of my hand to make sure it wasn't too hot. Then I picked up the baby and settled down into the rocking chair. Konjit gave me this quizzical stare. She turned to grope my breast, but she wouldn't get anything there. I touched the nipple of the bottle to the side of her mouth. Now if she had read the manual, she was to turn in the direction of the nipple and open her mouth and start to suck. But she had *not* read the manual. She started crying and pushing this foreign object, the bottle, away. She turned away from the bottle and her hands started flailing. At that moment, I really heard her cry! Great, she's breastfed, I thought. Of course, she would be breastfed. Most infants in Ethiopia were at that time. We fought this crazy game where I approached with the bottle and she pushed it away. After twenty minutes, I let her momentarily think I had given up. Jesus, I couldn't get her to take the bottle! How many new mothers had I taught to breastfeed?

I took a deep breath and warmed the bottle up again. This time, I took a thin blanket and wrapped her arms tightly so she couldn't push at the bottle. I took off my blouse and bra and then threw a shawl around my back. Then I picked her up again with bottle in hand. I dripped milk from the bottle onto my breast and she turned to grope my nipple. My God! The most excruciating pain descended on me when she glommed on to my breast and tried to suck the nonexistent milk from my nipple. When she opened her mouth a second time to clamp down, I quickly snuck the nipple of the bottle into her mouth. She first kind of gagged but then realized this strange bottle had warm milk that easily flowed from the nipple. She started suckling hard and fast but soon realized that wasn't necessary. Soon she had this contented look on her face and after 30 minutes her eyelids started to close, and she fell asleep. I picked her up to burp her and then placed her on her side in the crib. Please God, I hoped she was a fast learner and I wouldn't need to repeat this method again. I would have stayed in the rocking chair, but my stomach started to growl. I called room service for soup. And I wondered when she would be hungry again. Well, this baby liked to eat! Initially Konjit wanted formula every two hours, but she eventually settled down to every three hours.

Chapter 31

Ordered to Depart

Tuesday June 18

The next day, I went into the office after the Hilton sent me a babysitter for several hours. I thought I had best tell the national staff about my change of status. But when I walked in, I could see that Abebayehu had already informed everyone. They were excited and asking lots of questions and wanting to see the baby.

I said, "All in good time. I will bring her in. She's still small."

The phone rang, and Maryam—the head secretary—said, "Geneva on the phone. Why don't you take it in your office?"

I never liked early morning phone calls, and this one was no exception.

It was the head of the Communicable Diseases Unit, in Geneva.

"I don't know how to break this," he said, "but you need to leave Addis as soon as possible, certainly before the end of the month."

"Why? I don't understand," I said.

"The funds for your long-term contract haven't arrived from the US government. Headquarters borrowed funds from another program because we wanted to get going on the meningitis program, to ensure at least one country was prepared for the expected epidemics in 1991 or 1992. The Americans at USAID thought they'd have the funds by September 1990, but apparently your congressional budget has been delayed. Your six-month short-term contract is over at the end of June. If we had received the long-term funds, we would have automatically placed them on your contract and you'd have converted to long-term. I'm sorry, you have to leave."

"Well, this comes as a surprise! I didn't know I was on a short-term contract."

"I'm sorry, there are no funds for salary, health insurance, or danger pay. *You have to leave before the contract expires.* If it expires while you're in Ethiopia, you'll have no protection under the UN. Start closing down the Centre."

I gingerly replaced the phone in the cradle. I couldn't believe this shit! I was so close to adopting. How could I leave? If I left, everything had been a waste. It didn't look like I had a choice. But how could I leave my daughter in a place ravaged by war? I couldn't place her in an orphanage and hope to get back anytime soon. And what was the likelihood I could obtain a tourist visa to come back to Ethiopia? This place would be unsettled for the next two, four, six months or a year, easily.

I sighed and closed my eyes to keep from tearing up. I picked up the phone to call Monica.

"Bad news!" I said. "Geneva told me I have to leave, now, before the end of the month. Turns out the Americans have not come through with the long-term money for my contract. I have to leave before I lose diplomatic immunity, insurance, you name it. They never even told me I was on a short-term contract!"

"You're kidding, right?"

"I don't know what to do. I mean, Konjit is meant for me. How can I leave her here? Will I ever get back here? I'm supposed to close the EPR Centre. There's no way I can adopt her in less than two weeks. And no Ethiopians can leave the country!"

"What are you going to do, Connie?"

"I have no Goddamn idea." I said. "I guess I'm heading back to the Hilton right now."

I stopped in the secretaries' office and told them where they could reach me if I was needed.

I rushed back to my garden room and saw that Konjit was sleeping with the babysitter close by. I wasn't having difficulty feeding her now that she learned that taking a bottle was so easy. I kicked off my shoes and settled into the sofa. I needed to make another plan. For starters, I needed to figure out a good time to tell the national staff that I had to leave to go back to Geneva and the Centre would need to close down. There wasn't ever a good time for that. But first, I needed to know definitively whether I was leaving with my baby or leaving her behind.

I looked around the room and wished for a crackling blaze in the hearth. I missed the Ghion for that one consoling feature—the fireplace. I heard movement in the crib and whimpering from my daughter. My daughter! I took a prepared bottle out of the little fridge and heated it up on the single burner. When the bottle was warm, I took it out of the pan and tested it. Then I lifted up my daughter and cradled her in my arms. I sank down into the rocking chair.

She was staring intently at me as she chomped on the nipple, slurping milk. This was my daughter. I spoke quietly to her.

"I am your mother. Your birth mother will always be your birth mother, and she gave you life. But I am your mother because I chose to be. I worked hard for it. I submitted that dossier and waited the long wait for the Ministry to approve me. I knew you would come when everything was falling apart. I persuaded Geneva to let me stay on, even when the rebel army was about to invade, because I knew I had to stay in Addis. I chose love. I chose you. I am your *forever* parent."

Konjit suckled, unconcerned by the words I had to share with her in case we were separated, as tears rolled down my cheeks.

"I know a day will come when you'll say, 'I want to find my real parents.' But I will never stop loving you. I will bring you back to Addis one day to find your roots. You'll ask me some difficult questions, like 'Why did she give me up?' 'How could she give me up?' I also ask myself those questions. I can't know for sure, but an unmarried, pregnant Ethiopian girl of a certain standing would be an outcast to her family. And so, alone and afraid, with no one to give economic support, she tried hard to keep you. For three months she breastfed you, made you a handmade wool sweater, and somehow kept you from becoming malnourished like so many other infants I have seen. While under curfew, she hid in the forest surrounding St. George's Cathedral, waiting for the opportune time to place you just in front of the cathedral doors. She wanted you to be found by the priests, so she would know you would be well cared for. She didn't toss you in a garbage bin, or leave you by the side of the road, like some mothers do. I regret that I cannot give you many things. I regret that I know nothing about your family. I regret that you were born during the civil war. I regret the loss inherent in never truly knowing your Ethiopian heritage and culture, even as I try to learn more about it."

By now Konjit was asleep, but I had more to say.

"But in some ways, we're lucky. Amazingly, you look a lot like me. And because of the lack of a known family history, you're free from any undue expectations I might have to act like a 'Davis.' You're free to unfold into whatever person you want to be—an artist, an actor, even a doctor. You can decide. And while it's true you were adopted, and the school bully may tease you about this later, there are many kinds of families. You are more than the sum of a certain life event. You have the potential to do anything. I will fight to give you all the opportunities I can. *How you handle challenge and success will ultimately determine what you do with your life, not what happened to you early on.* The fact of being an orphan and being adopted does not define you. But, yes, your life will be profoundly different because you were adopted."

I arose from the rocking chair and laid my daughter in the crib. I knew what I had to do now. I had a plan.

Chapter 32

A Favor

The next day, I made an early morning call to Monica.

"Hey, Monica. Can I borrow your housekeeper for the next few days? I'll feel better about leaving Konjit in the care of someone I know. I'll need to run around and see folks," I said.

"Of course, Connie. As soon as she arrives, I'll tell her of her new duties and send her to the Hilton. Have you figured out what you're going to do?"

"I first have to contact Werke, but all government offices are still closed, so I'll be working on that! Thanks, Monica. You're a life saver." Because of the closure of government offices, I could not just drop into the MLSW to contact Werkesentayhu.

I called the office and let them know I was working from home at the Hilton. Then I had to wait until it was a decent hour to call someone. I usually called Werke at the Ministry, but he had given me his home landline. I picked up the telephone.

"Hello, Werke? This is Connie Davis. Everything all right in your area? Good. Ah, I don't know if Dr. Naviat told you, but I found my daughter. There's a bit of a problem, though. I need to see you as soon as possible, like right away!"

"I can meet you at my office tomorrow, Thursday, June 20. How about nine? I'll unlock the front door. Just push it and come in. I'll let the guard know to let you in," he said.

All right, now I had an appointment, but I needed to formulate my case. At that moment Nigist, Monica's housekeeper, knocked at the door. It was good to see a familiar face. I introduced her to my daughter, and then I showed her how to make formula. I also had a pail full of cloth diapers to finish washing out and then drying. At the time, disposable diapers in Nairobi were extremely costly and I had only bought one pack of twelve for use when we traveled. Cloth nappies (as the British would say) were the norm. Nigist retreated to the bathroom to wash the baby clothes and diapers. I had a very small patio where we could dry the diapers. Now I had time to resolve certain personal areas of indecision.

I needed to finally decide on a name for my daughter. While Cornelia was a family name, I never thought it did me justice. It sounded too formal and aristocratic for me and I always preferred my nickname—Connie. Once I had turned in my papers to formally adopt, I started to collect all the Ethiopian names I thought had a great sound and meaning. Yet, I also didn't want to saddle a child with an Ethiopian name that would cause frustration because it sounded too foreign, too long, or it didn't fit with our last name of Davis. Realistically, in the end, we would never be staying in Ethiopia, and I wanted a name that could withstand the bullies during noontime recess. It should also be fairly easy to pronounce.

It's not easy to pick a name. I thought of one day when I was looking at a pomegranate tree and I asked someone, what is this called in Amharic? And they said something that sounded like *romen* to me. I liked the sound of the name. So I played around with different spellings to get the sound and I ended up with

Romène. (Anyone French can pronounce it perfectly with an accent grave over the first *e* and a silent last *e*. For non-French speakers, it's pronounced "row-MEN" and accented on the last syllable.)

Now I had her first name. The middle name I found long ago—Alaana. It has many meanings—'cherished,' 'beauty,' 'serene,' and 'little rock' (beautiful to look at and rare, but also strong, tough, and unbreakable like a precious gemstone or jewel). The last meaning, 'little rock,' would actually turn out to be fairly descriptive of Romene. Tomorrow was a big day. I needed to persuade Werke to let me take Romene out of the country. That was the goal. It just wasn't so crystal clear to me how to effect that wish. I didn't stay up all night worrying. I would simply have to make it happen.

Abebayehu arrived at the Hilton bright and early the next morning. Nigist was already in the room.

"I'm off, Nigist. I should be back in a few hours," I said as I raced up the stairs.

And then I climbed into the car. "I need to go to the Ministry of Labour and Social Welfare," I said.

"I know where that is," Abebayehu said.

It was exactly as Werke had described. The guard waved us through the gate and when I reached the seemingly closed doors of the Ministry, I pushed and they opened. I carefully closed the door behind me. I went straight to Werke's office. He was waiting for me, sitting in one of the chairs in front of his desk. I sat down beside him.

"Dr. Davis, congratulations! You found your daughter," he said.

"I did. She's beautiful. But I need to talk about something else. WHO/Geneva called yesterday and said a complication had arisen, that I need to return to Geneva as soon as possible.

I want to discuss what options I have concerning my daughter. Addis is still in disarray. Most markets have not reopened, and it's not clear when they will. We are still under curfew. I know we agreed I would adopt in Ethiopia, but it's too risky to leave my daughter here when all services are suspended. I want to talk to you about making me a *foster parent*, so I can take Romene—that's her name—with me."

"We don't have this entity—foster parent—here in Ethiopia. You'll have to find a wet nurse to take care of her while you're gone."

I looked at him like he was crazy! "I'm supposed to go up to the top of Churchill Road and yell out, 'Any wet nurses for hire?' You've got to be out of your mind!"

I turned to face him head-on. I must have been out of my mind, because I have never done this to any government official before, but I grabbed the lapels on his sport jacket and said with a tremor in my voice, "Do you believe me that if I take my daughter, I will return to Ethiopia?"

He was surprised and a little fearful. "I believe you, Dr. Davis."

"And do you believe me that if for some reason beyond my control, I cannot return to Ethiopia, I will legally adopt her in the US?"

He nodded and said, "Yes, I believe you."

I picked up a ballpoint pen from his desk and thrust it into his hand.

"Then write this down word for word." I said. I stared off into the distance and dictated, "The Ministry of Labour and Social Welfare has no problem with Dr. Cornelia Estelle Davis taking her daughter—now get her name right—Romene Alaana Davis, with her to Geneva as she is called back on business."

I looked at Werke and said, "Call the judge, the one who only does adoption cases. Ask him to give you a date and docket number for her case before the court, and put that in the letter."

I jumped up and ran over to the wall calendar and flipped through the pages. I tapped my forefinger on the calendar.

"I will be back in Addis at the end of two months, three months at the outside, so set up the court proceedings in three months' time."

He stared at me, not moving.

"But, Dr. Davis, no Ethiopian can leave the country right now. They continue to search for Mengistu collaborators," he said.

"Don't you worry about that. I need the letter in Amharic. I'll send my driver to collect it in an hour, OK?"

He nodded in agreement. And I was off!

As I raced out of the building to find my car I thought, Davis, you just blew this! You threatened a government official. Oh my God, how could you grab the lapels on his sports jacket? Well, Werke would understand it was the pressure from the rebel takeover and the order to return to Geneva. At least he had seen me in better times. And I reflected back on his visit to Senegal. During my very first visit to Addis Ababa, when I had been checking out adoption, I had invited him to dinner if he actually got to attend an international workshop. I figured he would never get out of Addis! Boy was I surprised when he called me when he arrived in Dakar. I invited him and another Ethiopian participant at the workshop to come for dinner. We had a great time! Surely, he would remember that.

Now I needed to call in a favor. No one was in my garden apartment. I guessed Nigist had taken Romene out to get a little sunshine and a stroll. I picked up the phone and dialed the embassy.

The US consular officer picked up the phone.

"Hi, Mike, this is Connie. It's a miracle, but I found my daughter! However, Geneva has ordered me to depart, immediately." I took a deep breath. "I told you one day I would ask for a favor. Well, this is the day."

"Connie, I told you, I can't give her an American passport."

"I'm not asking for that. But someone in the embassy must know an official in the interim government with enough authority to make unilateral decisions. I need to speak to that person. I need an Ethiopian passport for my daughter."

Only silence on the other end.

"Are you telling me," I cried, "that no one in the US Embassy knows who's in charge in the new government?"

"I didn't say that," Mike said. "Let me call around. I'll get back to you this afternoon."

"I need to see him tomorrow at the latest," I said. "Thank you!"

I don't do waiting very well. I was pacing up and down in my room. Finally, the call came through.

"Connie, you have an appointment tomorrow at ten o'clock. Do you want me to go with you?"

"No, thanks. I appreciate the offer, but this is something I have to do alone."

I glanced at my watch. It was three in the afternoon. There was still enough time before curfew to go to the EPR Centre once the driver returned with the letter from the Ministry of Labour. I needed to write another letter on official WHO/EPR letterhead.

Friday June 21

Abebayehu, the driver, was at the Hilton at nine, and Nigist was already in the room cuddling Romene. I picked up the folder with the letter composed by Werke, and I checked that the letter I wrote as "Acting Director, WHO/EPR Centre" was also there. We left early, since I was not sure where the Ethiopian government office was located and the name of the official was also unknown to me. I kept rehearsing my lines, running them through my head as if I were in a play at the community theater. We found the building, and at each checkpoint I pointed to the name of the official I was to meet. A guard then escorted me to the reception area before the office. He indicated I could go through the inner door. Here goes nothing, I thought. And I took a deep breath.

I pushed open the door, entered, and looked at the person behind the desk. Unbelievable. I knew him. He was the one I had pleaded with to let Mebrahetu Gennet, the former WHO secretary and political prisoner, depart Ethiopia for humanitarian reasons. I rushed forward, smiling, and shook his hand and said, "We've met before, about Gennet."

He smiled and said, "Yes, Dr. Davis."

"This time, I'm here on a personal mission. I applied to adopt a child and, after meeting all the criteria, I was given permission in May by the Ministry of Labour and Social Welfare to look for an Ethiopian infant. I found my daughter only a few days ago, but WHO/Geneva has ordered me to return on business. I don't want to leave her here when things are still unstable. I have a letter from the Ministry of Labour that they have no problem with me taking *my daughter with me*." I then handed him the letter. I gave him a little time to read it. And then I continued.

"As the acting director of the WHO Emergency Preparedness and Response Centre, I am formally requesting that you issue an Ethiopian passport for my daughter, so she may leave with me."

I handed him the letter from the WHO/EPR Centre and rested my case.

He looked up at me and smiled and slowly bobbed his head. And then he read the letter I had written as acting director of the WHO/EPR Centre. He picked up the telephone and started talking in Amharic. Now I wished I had advanced a little further in my Amharic lessons. It seemed like an eternity, but he finally put down the receiver and said, "Monday, June 24, at four in the afternoon, you need to go to Immigration. Go around to the back of the building. You need to bring two black-and-white passport-size photos of your daughter, and you also need to bring your daughter. Give them the letter from the Ministry of Labour. They will issue her passport on Monday. Her name will be sent on to airport immigration that she is free to travel with you."

I tried to hold back the tears but couldn't.

"I don't know how to thank you, but thank you so much!"

And I left immediately, before he could change his mind.

Chapter 33

Whirlwind

Abebayehu could tell I was elated, he just didn't know why. I blurted out, "He said my daughter can have an Ethiopian passport and can leave with me!"

"Leave? Do you have to go, Dr. Davis?"

Oh crap, I forgot I hadn't told the staff. "Look, first things first. We need to return to the EPR Centre."

Then I called a hurried staff meeting of the national staff. I told them the disturbing news that I had to return to Geneva. There were contract problems. I was waiting to get word from Geneva about when the director, Dr. Suleiman, might be returning—since the airport was now open to flights. If he was returning soon, then the Centre would not need to close temporarily. Of course, staff were upset and worried.

Then I took the driver aside and said quietly, "You need to go to the photographer's studio on Churchill Road and find out where he lives. Search for him. This is important. Find him and ask him nicely to open the studio tomorrow at whatever time he wants. I can be there with Romene. Don't return until you find where he lives, and he agrees to open up his studio!"

OK, think, Connie. What do you need to do? I would need to call home and talk to my parents and update them on these recent events. Would they be surprised? I would be returning with a daughter. I had told them I planned to adopt, but when I went to Ethiopia this had been a rather nebulous plan. Now, it was reality.

I needed to contact the WHO national office (i.e., Monica) and ask them to arrange two one-way tickets for my return to Geneva and then on to San Francisco, California. If I got the Ethiopian passport on June 24, then we could safely plan to leave on June 26. I advised Monica that I thought children under one year of age traveled free. Then I called Mike at the embassy.

"Success," I cried. "I can take my daughter for an Ethiopian passport on Monday."

"Once you get the passport," he said, "send your driver with it to the embassy. I can put a six-month tourist visa on her Ethiopian passport."

"Thank you, Mike, for arranging the meeting with the official. Without embassy assistance, I would never have obtained that passport."

Then I called Karen Esteves at the WHO in Geneva to arrange lodging and other things in Geneva. I was happy Karen was my contact in the Communicable Diseases Unit. I had met her earlier in Geneva when I was first posted to Addis, so it would be easier to explain about bringing Romene with me.

"You are adopting an infant?" she said in amazement.

"Yes. They're giving her an Ethiopian passport, and the US is giving me a tourist visa, but I need assistance getting her into Switzerland!" I said.

"No problem. I'll get right on it with Immigration. As soon as you have her passport number, send it on to me," Karen said. "And you guys can stay with me in Geneva. It will be easier." Everything was finally falling into place.

And the rest was history. Abebayehu found the photographer, who opened the studio just for us, and who took the photos and developed them on Saturday. On Monday, I went to Ethiopian Immigration, where officials awaited us, and I gave them the black-and-white photos. It took them about an hour to produce the passport. Romene and I went back to the Hilton. The driver headed up to the embassy. I called Mike to alert him that the passport was on its way.

Then on Monday I brought Romene to the WHO/EPR Centre, so the staff could meet her. They all remarked how she looked a lot like me. I liked that. I picked up my ticket and per diem for travel, and we said our formal goodbyes. I looked around the office. I wondered if I would ever return? I sent off my last email as acting director to Geneva and suggested that if Dr. Suleiman was returning by the first week of July to let the Centre stay open, the WHO country office could pay the staff, and the operation could continue running.

Monica came to the Hilton before curfew fell. We reminisced about all we had gone through: the evacuation of the WHO expat staff, Mengistu fleeing the capital, the fall of Addis Ababa to the Tigrayans, the uprising against the US Embassy, retrieving the American family from Debre Zeit and the Flying Doctors from Nairobi coming to evacuate the child, the explosion of the underground munitions depot, and the call from Black Lion Hospital to come see a female baby. I had persuaded the interim government to give me an Ethiopian passport for my daughter, and they had agreed to let her leave. I was forever in their debt for letting my daughter depart with me. They had trust that I would return and adopt her in-country or in the US as appropriate. I hugged Monica and handed her the balance of my collection of antique silver necklaces and crosses to safeguard until my return. My intuition told me that Romene and I would return. We tried not to cry. Now I could only rely on the system. I worried about going through Immigration in the airport, but everything went smoothly. I relaxed only after the Lufthansa Airlines plane lifted off and retracted her wheels. We were off. Oh well, now what's next?

Chapter 34

The Mountains

I don't remember much of the plane ride on that late June day. Even though my seat was in the bulkhead, this plane was not equipped to hang a cradle there. A kind woman sitting next to me offered to hold Romene. I promptly fell asleep out of sheer stress. We had a tight connection in Frankfurt, but we were soon on the next flight for Geneva. Welcome to Switzerland! The Swiss are so thorough! They had Romene's name, and they stamped her entry and waved us through. Karen Esteves met us on the other side.

On the way to her apartment, she filled me in on the status of funding. The project was included in USAID funding, but they needed the US Congress to approve the annual appropriations bill. If I knew anyone in Washington DC, I should call them. Otherwise, I should take the time to enjoy maternity leave and let Geneva follow up. As far as WHO was concerned, they wanted me back in Ethiopia and we just needed patience. It was out of our hands, but the US needed a budget, so eventually it would pass.

Romene and I flew into San Francisco the next day, and my parents met us at the gate. My brothers and their families would greet us in Walnut Creek. I could then update everyone at the same time about the takeover of Addis and how I found my daughter. My older brother, Colbert, had a cabin at Kirkwood above Lake Tahoe and suggested they could take us up there to relax and enjoy the mountains. I definitely needed to de-stress.

"So, how long are you going to be in California?" my younger brother, Eddie, asked.

"Good question! It all depends on how long it takes the US government to get funds to WHO," I said. "I figure things will be clearer in two months. I'll either be returning to Ethiopia or looking for a new job."

I glossed over the details of the Tigrayan takeover of the capital, and I didn't dwell on the dangers of helping evacuate the Williams family from Debre Zeit. My family couldn't get over the fact that the Ethiopian government let me take Romene out of the country without adopting her. I just needed to get her back into Ethiopia, so I could adopt her there. I didn't want to even think of the problems and the costs of adopting her in the US.

When I look back now I remember those idyllic California summer days in the mountains. I bought a baby backpack, so I could easily hike and carry Romene on my back. Everyone wanted to hold her. I had no chance to practice being a single mom. Cheryl, my sister-in-law, wanted to hike with her through the woods. Rachel, my niece, was the perfect age for a babysitter. I had to practically stand in line to get a chance to feed her, since the grandparents were also up in the cabin at Kirkwood. Romene easily adjusted to all the new faces.

While in California, I thought it best to get a practicing pediatrician to give her a thorough physical and examination, to make sure we hadn't missed any slight detail. And she was in great physical shape.

In August, I got a welcome email from Geneva. They had received the funding for my long-term position from USAID.

They provided a date of August 12, when the packers would come to wrap up what I wanted to bring to Ethiopia. The rest could go into storage. Since I would be gone for two years, I needed to reflect on what items were easily available in Addis and what items I needed to bring with me. So I went on a shopping spree, primarily to get baby items like a stroller, Christmas and holiday gifts for when Romene was one and two years old, clothes, diapers, and formula. I bought items for myself like cosmetics, my special facial soaps, and creams. The only downer was that I didn't know where we would live, since I was certain the Debre Zeit house would not be renovated that quickly. And then, the house had memories I would just as soon forget.

Geneva sent the plane tickets. We would leave on September 15, 1991 and I would work for a week in Geneva. On September 21, we would arrive back in Addis Ababa, after exactly two months and twenty-five days out of the country. I was anxious to get back to the meningitis work. And I wanted to get the official adoption out of the way.

We were returning the same way we had come, through San Francisco on KLM Royal Dutch Airlines. I presented our tickets and passports to the lady behind the desk. When she got to the Ethiopian passport, she kept on flipping through the pages looking for something.

I said, "Give me the passport. I'll show you my daughter's multiple-entry visa for Switzerland!"

"I'm not looking for that visa," the airline representative said. "Where is the visa for Germany?"

"I'm not going to Germany," I replied. "I'm going to Geneva, and then on to Addis Ababa!"

"Well, this passport," she said, holding up the Ethiopian one, "*requires a transit visa* for Germany in order to proceed."

It hadn't even occurred to me that a transit visa was required for Germany. We didn't have one when we went through the first time. I could see I was going to have to pull rank here.

I smiled and said, "Could I speak to a supervisor, please?"

When the supervisor arrived, I said, "I'm Dr. Cornelia Davis. I work for the World Health Organization. I'm sorry, I was not aware Ethiopian passports needed a transit visa. I didn't have one on the outgoing trip. Here is my UN laissez-passer. My daughter is six months old. We are spending exactly one hour in Frankfurt, before we continue on to Geneva on official business. I request that you let us proceed, please."

The supervisor hesitated and then said, "I'm going to let you get on the plane this time, but you need to get rid of this passport and get an American one for your daughter. This passport will cause you a lot of trouble going forward." Under her breath she muttered, "Good luck in Germany."

And that's when I realized we would never easily travel to Europe or anywhere else with the Ethiopian passport. As soon as I returned to Addis, I needed to research how I could get an American passport for Romene. But at least we could get on the flight now.

The week in Geneva passed rapidly. I learned I had a new title at the EPR Centre—Chief of Preparedness Unit. Dr. Suleiman had returned just after I had left at the end of June. I let WHO resolve the issue of transit visas. They put Romene on my new United Nations laissez-passer travel document. This would present another complication for me. Anytime I wanted to travel outside Ethiopia with my laissez-passer, I had to take Romene with me. Oh, well, I'd figure that out later.

Chapter 35

Adoption

Romene and I arrived back at the Hilton, where it had all started less than three months earlier. The Hilton staff remembered us both. And, this time, I had a room on the third floor. The atmosphere in Addis was quite different. People were out in the streets. Traffic jammed the main roads and I heard that all the markets were open and busy. Everything seemed more hopeful. Monica was on her way over to bring me up to date and to see Romene. I thought to put through a call to Werke and let him know I was back!

"I knew you would return," he said. "Your court case is on October 11. Drop by this week whenever you have some time."

Monica filled me in on what had transpired while I was in California. Both of our respective directors had returned. Those who had been evacuated to Nairobi had returned. However, the US Embassy had not yet allowed their families to return.

High on my list of things to do were finding lodging outside the hotel and a *marmite*, an Ethiopian nanny. I definitely wanted to find a house before my household goods arrived. In the meantime, Monica's housekeeper, Nigist, offered to take care of Romene when I was at the office.

I couldn't wait to see my colleagues at the office. All had returned and, of course, had heard about my adopting Romene. I popped in to see Dr. Suleiman. He had returned the week following my departure. I told him I was eager to carry on the meningitis work. I would try and contact the government officials on the committee. I assumed they would still be in their positions. I sent out an email to see their availability to meet towards the end of the week. And then I started putting the finishing touches on the meningitis manual. At the end of the day, I dropped by the WHO national office to give them the shipping documents for the arrival of my household effects that were coming by air. I also needed to find out what my entitlements were regarding the import of a car. Since I now had a long-term contract, I could order something from Europe or Dubai.

I decided to drop by Werke's office at the Ministry of Labour and Social Welfare.

"You have everything you need for the court case?" I asked.

"There are still a few formalities. I need to post an announcement in the Addis Zemen newspaper about your daughter. This is the Ethiopian language newspaper, and it will state when Romene was found. It will also give the date and time of the court case, should the mother or another relative wish to oppose the adoption."

"I'm sorry, the mother can come forward at the court case and oppose the adoption? How often does this occur?" I asked.

"Not very often. I know of two instances," Werke said.

"What happened? What did the judge do?"

"Of course, it caused a commotion. The judge wanted to know why the child was initially abandoned and where the Ethiopian mother was in the intervening six months. Why was she coming so late to claim her child, and could she take care of him now? In the end, the judge ruled in favor of the foreign adoption."

Great! It had never occurred to me that at this late date the mother or a relative could still try to claim Romene. I wondered what the odds were that the birth mother would just happen to get the newspaper on the day of the announcement. How could she know if this was her baby or not? Could she even read the Amharic announcement? Clearly, I could do nothing. I simply had to wait for the court case in two weeks.

On the work side, WHO/AFRO requested that I travel to Brazzaville to update them on the status of the work in-country. I had scheduled a committee meeting to review with the members how far we had progressed in elaborating the guidelines. After that meeting and after the court case, I would go to Brazzaville.

And then Friday, October 11, 1991, arrived. I was to meet Werkesentayhu at the court. Romene did not have to be at the proceedings, and I felt it was better she remain behind. Werke had explained that the judge might be trying some other case before mine. The proceedings would be in Amharic, except for any questions the judge might ask me. When the judge called our case, Werke would stand and would present the salient features. According to Werke, the proceedings should go smoothly.

About one hundred people filled the room. The courts had been closed for several months, causing a backload of cases. Werke was already in the room and motioned me to come sit beside him. He whispered to me that we were next. After some fifteen minutes, our case started. Werke stood and proceeded to give an overview of my petition to adopt a now six-month-old infant. The judge looked at me and called my name. I stood up. I felt all eyes staring at me.

"Are you Dr. Cornelia E. Davis?" the judge asked.

"Yes, Your Honor, I am Dr. Davis."

The judge then said, "Dr. Davis is petitioning today to adopt an infant named Romene Alaana Davis. Is there anyone in this court who objects to the adoption going forward?"

I physically turned 360 degrees in the courtroom, almost daring anyone to be so brazen as to step forward. Silence.

And the judge ruled, "The adoption is granted to Dr. Cornelia Davis."

I gave a huge sigh. I think I had been holding my breath. Werke approached the bench to take a sheaf of documents from the judge. Then he came back and motioned me to follow him outside.

"Congratulations, Dr. Davis!"

I could finally breathe a little easier. "Thank you, for all your assistance."

"It will take my office about a week to register the adoption proceedings and to obtain a birth certificate for Romene. Once I have everything, I'll give you a call to come collect the documents."

I rushed back to the Hilton. Romene and I were invited to Monica's apartment to celebrate the official adoption with close friends. Later that night, as I rocked Romene to sleep in our room, I once again whispered to her.

"So today, Romene, you officially became my daughter. You are such an easy baby. You like loud music, will let anyone hold you if they rock you, and will take a bottle from anyone. As I pat your back as you fall off to sleep, I wonder what the future holds for you. I regret that you were born during the turbulent final days of Mengistu's regime. Somehow, I feel the civil unrest made it more difficult for your birth mother. I regret that I don't have a deep grasp of your Ethiopian culture, but I will do all I can to introduce you to it as time passes. I regret that your medical history is unknown. I will make sure you get all your preventive shots as required. Yet I take pleasure in the knowledge that we are embarking on a new life together. I take pleasure that you will have a wealth of opportunities that would never have been available to you if you remained an orphan in Ethiopia. Tonight, I feel confident that whatever lies ahead, we can handle it together!"

Chapter 36

Return to Normal

On returning to Addis, my overriding desire was to find permanent lodging. I didn't want to remain holed up in a hotel. I wanted my own home. I told everyone I knew, and even those I didn't, that I needed a house. In the end of September, I got a call from a woman pharmacist. She said she lived in the neighborhood called Old Airport, and that she would give up her house for rent and she and her family would look for other lodging. Old Airport was not that far from my work at the ECA, so I was eager to find out more information. I met Zemennesh after work one day at her house, which she had given me good directions to. Go to Mexico Square, and then head east and pass the Coptic church on your left. When the road takes a bend to the left, take the first dirt lane off to the right. The car was soon in front of the compound gate and the *zebanya* (guard) let us in. A big front yard meant space for two to three vehicles to easily park. The house had a long veranda that wrapped around the full length of the living and dining rooms, with four steps leading up to the front door. Zemennesh greeted me at the front door and invited me in.

Before she showed me the house, I thought it best to discuss my concerns in renting a private house from an Ethiopian, given all the rules and proclamations abounding. I explained that I had a long-term contract with WHO, but I had been waiting for official lodging since October 1990. I had adopted my daughter two months before, and I was shortly expecting an air shipment of household effects. I needed accommodations fast; yet I didn't want to break any rules and regulations. Zemennesh explained that she had heard about me from Ethiopian friends working in the HIV/AIDS division of the government. Her husband's family were former landowners. During the DERG administration, one of their two houses (the one next door), was appropriated by the government. They were left with this one, in which they lived. They had gotten their older son out of Ethiopia when he was accepted at the University of California, San Francisco School of Medicine.

"That's where I studied medicine," I said excitedly.

She smiled and nodded.

It was extremely hard for them to get funds out of Ethiopia to support their son. Some friends had helped initially, but they clearly needed to come up with other plans. She was aware that money, particularly US dollars, were not to be provided in Ethiopia. And this wouldn't help anyway, since they had no way to get it to their son. But if I liked the house, I could deposit funds in their son's bank account in San Francisco each month. This way, neither of us would technically be breaking the law.

"Well, let's take a look at the house," I said.

And she took me on a tour. It was a two-story affair. On the ground floor was the kitchen with a door out the side, leading to the garden. The front living room opened into a foyer to the front door, and led to the dining room. Towards the back of the living room was a small bedroom. The living room had an immense working fireplace. On the second floor were three bedrooms, two of which had attached baths. The master bedroom was quite large and had a fair amount of closets and storage. A small backyard was behind the house. The basement included servants' quarters and a storage area. It was much larger than the previous rental on the Debre Zeit Road. The neighborhood seemed quiet. A house sat on either side, but there were open fields as one went farther down the lane. I was favorably impressed. There was plenty of room for me to have a full-time live-in nanny for Romene. It was relatively close to my work and would allow me to come home at lunchtime to play with Romene.

"I feel bad about kicking your family out of the house," I said.

"Actually, you would be doing us a great favor. We were at our wits end on how to get funds to our son in the States. Do you like the house?" she asked.

"I love it! When could we move in?"

"We have found a rental very close," Zemennesh said. "You could move in by October 15."

To cement the deal, she offered her *marmite*, Missah, who had helped her raise her three children. Now her youngest was fifteen and didn't need a nanny, but Missah had stayed on with them; she had left her own family as a teenager, so she had nowhere to go.

"It would actually help us. Since things are tight, Missah would stay with you and you would pay her directly. The only drawback is that she only speaks Amharic," she said.

"I guess that would help me improve my Amharic!" I said.

And so we agreed on the spot, both of us thinking we got the better deal! I found an experienced *marmite* who worked for a landowner family, and so would know the basic hygienic rules of child caring. I would need to go over my rules, but I had worried how I would find someone. I also inherited their guard, who would stay at the house and I would pay him directly. Now, I only had to find a cook. Monica had already volunteered to stay in the house to oversee the activities whenever I had to travel for work. Now I just had to buy equipment and supplies for the house. The kitchen was spacious but was essentially bare. It had no stove, no refrigerator, and few cabinets. The owners could not leave items like that behind, which were costly for Ethiopians to replace. A store in town that catered only to diplomats sold imported kitchen equipment, furniture, and the like, but at a reasonable price. And I could easily find beds and mattresses. Monica even offered me her cook, Nigist, with the understanding that any time she was having a party, Nigist was to help. What a relief. I could move out of the hotel in two weeks and, once settled in, turn my attention to meningitis again.

Right after the adoption proceedings, I left for Brazzaville to update the WHO Regional Office for Africa on progress. The committee had developed two manuals, one on the prevention and control of meningitis and another for responding to outbreaks. They would not be finalized until after the districts had provided feedback at a country-wide meningitis workshop in January 1992. But my main concern was they would sit in a drawer unless the laboratory supplies for diagnosis, the vaccines, and the antibiotics—particularly oily chloramphenicol—were provided to Ethiopia.

I wanted to get the discussion started about how the regional office would supply countries once they developed their guidelines. If we expected countries to stop the outbreaks immediately, they needed these supplies *before* an outbreak occurred and pre-positioned throughout the country. The regional program needed to put a line item in their budget request to Geneva, so as countries developed their guidelines they would be assured to get the supplies they needed.

I was eager to return to Addis Ababa. The WHO country office had notified me that my belongings had arrived and just needed to clear customs. So as soon as I arrived back, I would have household goods to unpack and to get settled. I also talked with the priest at Holy Savior Catholic Church about the christening (baptism) for Romene on Saturday, November 2, and then a party at the house on Sunday, November 3. It was going to be a rush to get everything prepared. And I still needed to select the godparents. Of course, Monica was the top choice for godmother. I needed to figure out who I could ask to be the godfather.

Jan Evans was working at the Ministry of Mines for about a year before I arrived in Ethiopia. He and his wife Carolyn were living in the Ghion when I arrived—like we all were at one time. The Evans were always friendly to me and included me whenever they were going exploring outside Addis. We often headed to Mount Entity, the highest peak overlooking Addis Ababa. The mountain was densely covered by eucalyptus trees imported from Australia during the reign of Menelik II, and mostly planted during Emperor Haile Selassie's reign. It made a nice Sunday outing, and one could find restaurants or take fixings for a picnic. At the time, I didn't have a car, and they were generous to invite me on those outings—which were a nice respite from the city. The Evans were evacuated with the nonessential UN staff that went off to Nairobi for what turned out to be three months. But they were back in town and were excited to be a part of the christening ceremony.

The actual christening at the Holy Savior Church was an intimate affair, with only Monica as godmother, my friend Jan as godfather, Jan's wife (Carolyn), Maryam (the EPR secretary), Romene, and myself. The main actors were actually Monica and Jan, who took turns holding Romene as the holy water was poured over her head. Romene let out a scream to wake the dead, which was surprising coming out of so tiny a person. I wondered if in the US they warmed the holy water or at least let it get to room temperature. Immediately following the baptism, we went into the rectory, where Romene's name, date of birth, and baptism name were written in the big book. I was also given the baptismal certificate to take at that time. It was only later, several months later actually, that I had time to read the document closely. It seems in Ethiopian tradition, and due to high infant mortality and because people may live some distance from the church, that the infant received the confirmatus rites at the same time as the baptism.

Thanks to Maryam, we held a traditional Ethiopian christening party at my house. Romene and I had on beautiful traditional Ethiopian dresses with intricate embroidered hems. And I had to perform the coffee ceremony, an integral part of Ethiopian social and cultural life. Coffee is offered when visiting friends, during festivities, or as a daily staple of life. An invitation to attend a coffee ceremony is considered a mark of friendship or respect, and it is an excellent example of Ethiopian hospitality. Performing the ceremony is almost obligatory in the presence of visitors, and although I was not expected to perform all the various intricate steps, I had to at least start it, and Maryam took over the intricate parts. Be aware about accepting to attend the coffee ceremony, because it can take a few hours!

There is a long, involved process that starts with setting up a shelf-like box of furniture called a *rekbot*, which Maryam lent me. The *rekbot* holds all the ceremonial apparatus such as the handle-less cups, called *cini*, and the special pots used to brew the coffee. The *rekbot* is arranged upon a bed of long, scented grasses. The roasting of the green coffee beans is done in a flat pan over a tiny charcoal stove, the pungent smell mingling with the heady scent of frankincense and myrrh that is always burned during the ceremony. I was allowed to perform the task of roasting the beans, since that was the easiest part of the ceremony. When the coffee beans turn black and shining and the aromatic oil is coaxed out of them, they are ground by a pestle and a long-handled mortar. Maryam mixed the ground coffee with spices and poured the mixture into a pot known as a *jebena*, which had hot water simmering in it.

The coffee grounds are brought to a boil. After brewing, the coffee is put through a sieve several times. The *jebena* is usually made of pottery and has a spherical base, a neck and pouring spout, and a handle where the neck connects with the base. When it's time to pour the coffee, the long, thin, narrow spout acts as a strainer and keeps the grounds from flowing out. The hostess pours the coffee for all participants by moving the tilted, boiling pot over a tray with small *cini* from a height of one foot, without stopping until each cup is full. To do this feat takes years of practice, and I turned this part of the coffee ceremony over to Maryam. The coffee grounds are brewed three times: the first round of coffee is called *awel*, the second *kale'i*, and the third *baraka*—which means 'to be blessed.' It is imperative to consume at least three cups, as the third round is considered to bestow a special blessing.

Coffee, or *bunna*, in Ethiopia is taken with plenty of sugar but no milk. A transformation of the spirit is said to take place with the ceremony. And coffee holds a sacred place in the country. An ancient Ethiopian proverb states "*coffee is our bread*"! As I looked out over my invited guests, I reflected on Romene's christening and how the coffee ceremony was cementing our relationship to the Ethiopian culture.

For those who preferred a slightly stronger brew, there was plenty of St. George's beer to wash down the *doro wat*—spicy Ethiopian chicken stew. Maryam also located traditional musicians to play folk songs on their instruments. I hired tables and chairs to place in the front garden, and the weather was perfect. It was tradition to invite the priest to the festivities, so Father James was there. Key guests were my compatriots, who were essential staff that stayed behind during the takeover of the capital only seven months previously. And of course, the friends who had returned from Nairobi.

It was almost unfathomable to envision all that had happened in my first year in Addis Ababa. As I gazed at my friends enjoying the day, I remembered all the convoluted steps that had brought us to this moment: submitting the completed adoption dossier, Monica and me going to the police station to get the certificate of good moral standing, the Tigrayan rebels entering the city, evacuating the Williams baby from Debre Zeit, surviving the underground explosion of the munitions depot that blew out the roof and windows of my first rental house, getting permission from the Ministry of Labour to look for an infant, answering the call from Dr. Naviat to come to Black Lion Hospital, receiving the other call from WHO/Geneva that I had to leave immediately, petitioning the Ethiopian government to provide a passport for Romene, returning to California to visit my parents and family, and finally going to the adoption proceedings in Addis in October 1991.

I reflected on how much I had grown over the past year. It was easy to doubt myself when facing what seemed like insurmountable challenges. Yet, it was at those junctures, when I was at my lowest, that I remained persistent and determined. I remembered a quote I loved. "*Risking is better than regretting.*" I didn't want to look back on my life one day and wonder "what if." I was proud of myself for the calculated risks I took and the amazing reward that was my daughter.

I was looking forward to a little down time with Romene, and bonding. But then I got a call from AFRO about a meningitis outbreak in northern Nigeria. They needed assistance right away.

Chapter 37

Another Outbreak

Nigeria! This definitely wasn't East Africa. I did not want to go to Nigeria. I would have to fly into the infamously corrupt Lagos airport—Murtala Muhammed International Airport. Technically this would not be my first time there!

When I had worked as the regional epidemiologist in the Combating Childhood Communicable Diseases Project in Côte d'Ivoire in 1988, I had been flying on an Air Afrique flight from Malawi to Abidjan. We made an unscheduled fuel stop at the Lagos airport. The plane remained on the tarmac for the entire refueling. I couldn't even see the airport. No one got off the plane. When we finally arrived in Abidjan, half of the passengers—including myself—were missing their luggage! For one year, I fought with Air Afrique to reimburse me for the suitcase and its contents. For one year, I always used to check the lost and found luggage. Exactly one year later, Air Afrique finally provided me the cost of my suitcase only. So, I did not have fond memories of Lagos. I was not looking forward to this adventure.

The WHO Country Office for Nigeria sent me explicit directives about how I was to get off the plane, locate my luggage as priority, go through Immigration *but not let go of my passport*, and then come out into the arrivals hall. I was *not* to let any airport luggage handler "help" me with my bag. I was to locate the WHO driver, who would be in uniform. I was to ask for his identification, which would be in English. I was *not* to leave in any unauthorized airport taxi, but *only* in the WHO vehicle. These directives did nothing to dispel the rampant rumors surrounding the Lagos airport. Pickpockets, con artists, gangsters, and thieves—anyone who went through the Lagos airport had a tale to tell about a run-in with one of these.

What first hit me was the suffocating heat inside the terminal. I passed the first test, which was to get my passport stamped without releasing it from my hand. Then on to baggage. I stationed myself right where the bags shoot out on the antiquated carousel, and I grabbed my bag before anyone else could. I placed it on the trolley and headed for the door. After I went through the door, there was no arrivals hall. I was immediately confronted by five hundred bloodshot eyes clamoring to provide assistance. Everyone was yelling at me.

"You put your Goddamn hands on my trolley, I'll kill you!" I said to no one in particular.

A uniformed man approached me. "Dr. Davis, I am the WHO driver, here are my credentials," he said.

I quickly looked them over and returned them.

He then told me, "I have to go back into the terminal. The other doctor I was picking up handed over his briefcase with his passport and credit cards to a 'guy in a uniform,'" the WHO chauffeur said. "Can you wait right here? Do not let anyone take anything from you! I'll be back in fifteen minutes."

He took my suitcase off the trolley and had me straddle the bag. I clutched my hand purse to my chest and put the long strap over my neck. I put on my fiercest "don't you fuck with me" stare. And I waited. I must have looked like the perfect target. Charlatans and drug-addicted rascals known as area boys approached. If I could have collected 5 USD for everyone saying, "*Sister, please, I have two small children at home, let me help you find a nice taxi . . .*" I'd be rich right now!

"Touch my bag and I'll scream!" I warned them all.

The driver eventually came back. He called the office to send out an admin officer to help. I was traumatized just thinking about the other doctor who hadn't yet emerged from customs. That could just as well have been me. Lagos was scary as hell. Suspicion permeated the air, trust was nonexistent, and fear kept me alert. I simply wanted to get to the hotel and get a good night's sleep. Things had to be better in the morning.

Another WHO car picked me up in the morning. I was provided a good orientation and found out the outbreak was in the north—Muslim territory. I needed to fly up to Kano. That meant I had to face the Lagos airport again.

"Don't worry, Dr. Davis, the WHO driver who goes to the airport is also listed as an *official facilitator*. He will go in with you, make sure you have the right boarding card, and see you to the plane," the WHO admin officer said.

Things proceeded like clockwork. The car arrived on time, we got the boarding pass for the private commercial plane with no hassle, and he took me to the boarding gate.

"Thanks, Mohammed. You were a great help, but you don't have to stick around any longer," I said.

"I'm to see you on the plane. So, when they call your flight, we'll line up at the gate. When they check you through, I'll go also, and you will give me your boarding pass. I'll run ahead and get in line just in front of the plane," he said.

This was decidedly strange. Sometimes the flights were oversold but they still gave out boarding passes to all who showed up. If you wanted to ensure that you actually got on the plane and had a seat, you needed to be first in line before the plane on the tarmac and first on the plane! And that's how it went. Once my boarding pass was checked by the airline representative and I walked through the gate, the WHO facilitator took my boarding pass and sprinted on ahead to the plane. He was actually third in line before the plane. As I walked up, we exchanged places and I was third in line. He handed me my boarding pass and waited to see me walk up the steps to the plane.

"Have a good trip, Dr. Davis," he called as I entered the plane.

I was exhausted before the plane even left Lagos. I hoped Kano was easier to navigate. I was met by the district health officer and taken to the District Health Office to receive an orientation.

The outbreak was occurring in outlying areas between Katsina and Kano. They had taken samples of lumbar fluid from the first patients, so we knew what we were dealing with. They were using IV medication, but clearly procuring single-dose intramuscular oily chloramphenicol would simplify treatment. They had vaccines, but the populace was resisting them. Even with administrating childhood vaccinations, the northern populace had a prolonged and protracted distrust of vaccinations, and false rumors and untruths always circulated. To try and gain the population's trust, we needed to obtain cooperation and support from the emir.

In pre-colonial times, the emir was the head of an emirate, vested with legislative, executive, and judicial power. He was an absolute ruler. That is, the emir was supreme in decision making and whatsoever he ordered must be carried out, with the understanding that he was following Sharia law. Therefore, the emir was both the political and religious head. In modern times, the democratically elected government clashed with the emirs.

While the emirs commanded considerable traditional allegiance in certain areas, their non-elective status made them a target by local politicians and other critics. But clearly, if we could get the emir of Kano to encourage the people to get vaccinated, it would be easier to bring the outbreak under control. And so, with the district medical officer, we asked for an audience with the emir. We were able to meet with one of his deputies and stressed that the meningitis vaccine protected against the disease. And wonder of wonders, we were able to get a statement from the emir encouraging the population to protect themselves and their families.

Most meningitis outbreaks occurred in northern Nigeria. While meningitis outbreaks occurred year-round, certain environmental factors played a significant role in making this particular outbreak an epidemic. From December to May, the dry, brittle wind called the *harmattan* blows across northern Nigeria. This makes droplets of saliva easily transmitted from person to person, while living in tight quarters. Vaccination would be the only thing to bring this outbreak under control. I headed back to the capital, Lagos, and presented the report to the WHO representative. I sent an urgent email to Geneva requesting oily chloramphenicol and additional vaccines.

Chapter 38

Bonding

Addis Ababa was one of the few capitals where I worked in which I could go home for lunch and play with my daughter, and I could still get back to the office in time for afternoon appointments. And even though the capital and I had a rough start, in hindsight, Addis now gave us a tranquil family environment. There were five of us total living in the compound. Besides my daughter and me, there was Missah, the *marmite*; Nigist, the housekeeper/cook; and Duress, the guard.

Once all the nonessential staff returned from Nairobi, Monica arranged a belated baby shower for Romene. I don't know where my friends found their gifts, but they were charming. Favorites included a huge stuffed camel for Romene to ride, a "dragon" rocking horse, disposable diapers, hard-to-find baby clothes (which enterprising souls picked up in Nairobi), and candles and incense. Someone also gave me this clever *A First Year Calendar with Stickers*. The stickers said things like "First Smile," "First Tooth," and "Says Mama," and you could place them on the calendar. We were relaxing in the mountains at the Kirkwood cabin when Romene first started saying "mama." And a little before six months old she started holding her own bottle.

It was during the lunchtime hour sitting on the porch of the Old Airport house that I could just relax and hold Romene and hear the birds chirping in the garden. After taking the bottle, Romene normally fell off to sleep and I would hand her over to Missah to take her upstairs to sleep. And I could head back to the office.

When I came back in the evenings, Missah was there with Romene to greet me. They let me go upstairs to change into jeans and a T-shirt. Nigist was in the kitchen putting on the finishing touches to dinner. I could make a gin and tonic and then get Romene so we could enjoy the sunset. As I look back on those times, I realize how easy it was being a single parent overseas. I had plenty of help that would not have been affordable in the US. Nigist did all the grocery shopping and cooking for the staff and me. I bought an electric *injera* maker, so it was easy for Nigist to make a large lunch for the staff. She even taught me how to make *injera* from scratch. But it does take some skill to pour out the batter on the electric plate and to know that when the little bubbles appear on the surface, it's time to lift the bread off the pan. Nigist was also the housekeeper, and those onerous chores of cleaning the bathrooms, making the beds, and cleaning the living room were not on my shoulders. Missah took care of everything to do with Romene, from washing her clothes and nappies to feeding her when I was at work. Until Romene started sleeping through the night, she would help with the nighttime feedings. I didn't feel the full weight and the stress of single parenting until some eight years later, when I returned to the States for a three-year period.

On the weekends, I fell back into the routine that I had before Romene arrived. On Sundays after church, we would head to the Hilton for brunch with the usual suspects. I had bought one of these infant-to-toddler rockers in the States, that converted to an infant seat. Depending on the venue, Romene could sit among my friends on a chair or in a booth. She actively watched all the participants. My friends insisted I bring her to parties. She was an "easy" baby, and new faces didn't scare her or cause her to cry. She loved music and enjoyed "dancing" in my arms to the beat of a popular rock-and-roll melody. The curfew had been lifted by now, so I no longer had to barrel down the road to get home. But I had my own curfew. It was tiring being a new mother! I even developed "tennis elbow" in my right arm from the repeated lifting and lowering of my daughter from the crib.

Before I knew it, Romene's first Thanksgiving was just around the corner. In those days, it was difficult to find a real turkey in Addis—unless you were somehow associated with the US Embassy, which brought them in from Nairobi. Luckily, we were invited to the Consul's house for dinner! I had much to be thankful this November day. And Christmas was coming.

I went shopping as before, in the special markets set up for Western Christmas. The difference was that I had Romene in the baby sling with me. I found a place that sold live Christmas trees, and I bought a small spruce tree. I found twinkling tree lights in the market. The various NGOs made special ornaments for the tree, and it was in Addis that I started collecting ornaments from each country where I worked. Monica was giving a party on Christmas Eve, so Nigist went up to help her prepare. Romene and I went up for the festivities. This was our first Christmas party. And Monica came over on Christmas morning to help us open our Christmas presents.

I experienced the provisional government by what it was *not* doing. It wasn't in your face, making pronouncements left and right. They let the bureaucrats run the normal workings of the government. I didn't see soldiers in the streets, fuel was readily available for cars, and food was plentiful in the markets. And it finally dawned on me that I no longer heard gunshots in the night.

Then Ethiopian Airlines announced it was restarting, and the maiden flight—a day trip—was to the rock-hewn churches of Lalibela on Dec 29, 1991. Ethiopian Airlines was sending a small plane at first, to check out the state of the dirt-packed runway and how the small hotels and lodgings had survived the war. I immediately rushed to Ethiopian to get my name on the inaugural flight. During the war, I had greatly feared I might never see those World Heritage sites. The Lalibela monolithic rock-hewn churches had always held a fascination for me from the time I first learned about them (and Ethiopia), when I was in graduate school. Subsequently, in the midst of the Ethiopian civil war, the main tourist areas—comprising the historic sites of Lake Tana and the Blue Nile Falls, Aksum, Gonder, the Simien Mountains, and Lalibela—were off-limits. So this was a big deal.

Lalibela lies in a mountainous region in the heart of Ethiopia, some four hundred miles north of Addis Ababa. Eleven monolithic medieval churches were carved out of rock. They are the biggest monolithic temples in the world. Their construction was attributed to King Lalibela, who set out in the twelfth century to erect a *New Jerusalem*, after Muslim conquests halted Christian pilgrimages to the Holy Land. Lalibela flourished after the decline of the former Aksum Empire.

The flight left early in the morning from Bole Airport and I think all thirty of us felt we were privileged and truly lucky to be on the flight. There was no tour guide, so I had to read up about Lalibela on my own. The small plane landed on a short dirt-packed runway, some distance from the village. The pilot reminded us that we needed to return to the plane by two p.m., or we would be staying there for a long while. And then he pointed us in the general direction of the town. The locals, who hadn't seen tourists for three years, quickly surrounded us. An adolescent boy, around sixteen, latched on to a small group from the plane. He guided us to the main cluster of churches and showed us how to get down through the passageways to approach the entrance to the churches. And then he left us to our own devices to explore.

As we only had four hours on the ground, it was impossible to visit all eleven churches. I only made it to two of them. One of them was *Biete Giyorgis* (Church of Saint George), thought to be the most finely executed and best-preserved church of the rock-hewn temples. I only have slides of the exteriors of the churches, so I suspect one of the priests told us not to take photos of the interiors.

The churches were not constructed in the traditional Western way (placing stones on top of each other), but rather were hewn from one solid rock each—monolithic blocks. These blocks were further chiseled out, forming doors, windows, columns, various floors, roofs, etc. This gigantic work was further completed with an extensive system of drainage ditches, trenches, and ceremonial passages, some with openings to hermit caves and catacombs.

According to legend, an angel came and asked King Lalibela to build the churches. Men and angels worked together to construct them, the men working through the day and the angels working through the night. Legend claimed that the churches were built in twenty-four years, however, archaeologists consider this impossible. Even today, accomplishing this work in that short of time,—using carbon steel–tipped chisels and diamond blades—would be remarkable.

Lalibela was still a major pilgrimage site for followers of the Ethiopian Orthodox Church, and its eleven churches were among the finest of Ethiopia's nearly two hundred rock-hewn churches. These churches were neither ruins nor museums, but were used continuously for ceremonies, although several were currently showing the effects of earthquakes, flooding, and environmental damage. Precise dating for the complex and its components had yet to be determined, although scholars generally agreed that the churches were constructed in four or five phases between the seventh and thirteenth centuries.

The midday sun was hot and bright, and after tramping around several churches we were hungry. So we looked for shade under a tree. We had been told to bring water and lunch with us, as we would not have time to go into the village. I pulled out my water bottle and a ham and cheese sandwich that Nigist had made. By the time we finished eating, we could see some of the tourists that were on the plane heading back to the runway. Without a guide to point out architectural features and other aspects of the churches, I'm sure I only had a cursory idea of what these churches meant to the population. However, my overriding impressions were ones of marvel, amazement, and uniqueness. Lalibela remains an almost mystical experience stamped forever in my psyche, never to be forgotten. The tiny airplane lifted off into the heavens and circled once over the cluster of churches. We headed back to Addis. The pilot had one more treat for us. He announced that his flight pattern would go over the Blue Nile Falls. From my window seat, I had an unobstructed overhead view of the waterfalls known as *Tis Abay* in Amharic, meaning "great smoke." Breathtaking!

Chapter 39

New Citizen

I was hopeful the new government would let go of some of the mistakes of the old DERG. I think everyone just wanted to give peace a chance.

Western Christmas had come and gone, and we passed the New Year.

Then one day, I received an email from USAID that they were sending a consultant to do a mid-term evaluation of their support to the EPR Centre. They had supported it before I was hired as the Chief of Preparedness.

The USAID consultant came for about a week in May. He seemed concerned that I was doing activities outside my scope of work. I was in charge of *preparedness*, but I was also covering response aspects. All the outbreaks I assisted outside of Ethiopia were technically helping countries respond to an epidemic. This was the work of the Response officer which, at the time, the Centre didn't have.

In June, the director of the EPR Centre, Dr. Suleiman, announced at the weekly staff meeting that he would be moving on. His family had never returned to Addis after the events of the Tigrayan rebel takeover. I was informed that I was once again "acting director" until a new director arrived. I didn't let the title "go to my head," since the reality would soon set in. It simply meant more work and high-level meetings, but with the same pay scale. But I was working on other plans, so to speak.

My first year as Chief of Preparedness was quickly ending, and I had annual leave coming up. I was dreading crossing international borders with Romene's Ethiopian passport, so I was working with my younger brother, Ed (the lawyer), about trying to "expedite" naturalization for Romene.

According to the adoption policy of the time, in order to start the naturalization process for Romene we had to return to the States, and after living there for *seven* years I could start the process. But I was never planning to return to the US. I loved working internationally and I planned to continue looking for opportunities in immunization policy or infectious diseases, hopefully in francophone countries. I didn't want to lose my facility in French. At the same time, I needed to obtain an American passport for my daughter. I ran into some old hands in the UN family, and they told me something about *expedited naturalization* that was given to Americans in the UN system who had adopted children. Given that UN personnel were posted worldwide and seldom in their home countries, this seemed a brilliant option. My younger brother, the lawyer, was to investigate and get back to me.

Ed told me he had a friend who worked in immigration law. His lawyer friend, Richard, was willing to investigate the criteria for expedited naturalization and he was doing it "pro bono." I was extremely grateful that Richard offered his services to help me. He prepared and submitted all the papers to prove I qualified under the rules, and Romene and I had an appointment at the US Citizenship and Immigration Services (USCIS) San Francisco Field Office, the first week of my vacation.

It felt strange to be a single parent sitting in this big hall in Immigration surrounded by couples, families, and single folk.

"Dr. Davis?"

I heard my name and jumped up, pushing Romene in her stroller. I introduced Romene to the immigration officer and he got down quickly to the task.

"Your papers are all in order. How is Addis Ababa now?" he asked.

I explained that things had calmed down. I had plenty of work to do in infectious diseases.

"Are you ready to take the oath of citizenship for your daughter?"

"Ready and willing," I said as I stood up and raised my right hand. And I repeated, "*I pledge allegiance to the flag of the United States of America . . .*" as if hearing the words for the first time. Then I signed her naturalization papers and, bam, she was an American! Relief!

"Can I apply for a passport for Romene right away?" I asked.

And he handed me the application form and said, "Fill it out right now. You'll get it in about five to six weeks."

That meant we would have the passport for our return. I wouldn't have to request special transit visas and all the rest. *Yes!* Life was good.

Chapter 40

The Next Chapter

When we arrived back in Addis from my annual leave, I found that Dr. Suleiman had already left. I was once again acting director of the EPR Centre. Dr. Suleiman had been working with the Organization of African Unity (OAU) to put pressure on the Ministries of Health to be more proactive in preventing infectious diseases, particularly epidemics. Epidemics were potentially destabilizing for countries, and it always ended up requiring more money to control an outbreak than to prevent it in the first place. So opportunities existed to present key policy issues on a higher level than I usually worked, to bring additional allies to bear on controlling communicable diseases and especially meningococcal meningitis. A key component of the director's job was fundraising. And that was fundraising for the whole Centre, and not just meningitis. The EPR Centre was working on natural and man-made disasters, humanitarian issues, meningitis epidemics, and the use of geographic information systems.

In fact, the national HIV/AIDS program had already approached the WHO/EPR Centre to help them look at their data spatially and to present their findings visually. That way, they would be able to help the Ethiopian government understand the rapidly escalating problem of HIV/AIDS in the country. They even had money to pay the Centre to put their data in an easy-to-understand format! And we were happy to oblige.

In the meantime, Geneva found additional funds for Ethiopia, and I was able to work with the Ministry of Health to make the guidelines for prevention and control of meningitis operational. The Ministry was busy pre-positioning vaccines and medicines and planning to train the health workers. I would assist them in the training that would roll out in the first quarter of 1992.

One day in July 1992, a plain white envelope arrived on my desk, on top of the other official mail. The return address showed it was sent from the UK. I opened the letter with some curiosity. It was from Patricia Williams, and the memories flooded back of me heading to Debre Zeit in the ambulance to rescue the infant with a bullet lodged in his spine. I had often wondered what had happened to baby John, and whether he was paraplegic.

"Dear Dr. Davis," the letter began. "I remember with fondness and gratitude that you came to Debre Zeit to give aid to our John." She went on to write that, when the plane eventually got to Nairobi, they were rushed to the Nairobi Hospital. The ER medics said they were surprised to see that, after all those days in the field, the wound was clean and free of sepsis! The Williamses gave me all the credit for that. However, I think God had a hand in it also. They only stayed two days in Nairobi, while the doctors stabilized the baby and then medically evacuated him to London. The surgeons there elected to observe initially and not do any surgery until later. Once the swelling regressed, they noticed slight movement in the lower legs. John had, and was continuing with, intensive rehabilitation and he had slowly regained the use of his lower limbs. With the help of braces, he was learning to walk! She wanted to make sure I heard about this good news. I sat in my office, and the tears flowed freely down my cheeks.

I glanced through the rest of the mail. The WHO/EPR Centre was actively recruiting for a director to take over from Dr. Suleiman. My immediate worry was to determine if I should continue in preparedness activities in Ethiopia, or if I should look for job opportunities elsewhere. In the world of international public health, monies for primary health care and immunizations were rapidly decreasing and more funds were going into the new disease of the month—HIV/AIDS. More and more of my colleagues in immunization were reporting that they were going over "to the dark side," meaning they were taking positions in HIV/AIDS.

Initially, I had no interest in HIV/AIDS. More children died from malaria and diarrhea than from AIDS! I felt it was shortsighted to decrease or take funds away from programs that were tackling the major problems and had programs and drugs that effectively targeted those problems. At that time, in the early throes of the HIV/AIDS epidemic, all anyone could do was to diagnose and provide supportive care and then watch the child die. My friends who had already made the switch to HIV cautioned me.

"Right now, while everyone is struggling to find out about HIV/AIDS and how it spreads and how to prevent it, programs are scrambling to find experienced epidemiologists," they said. "After five years, HIV/AIDS programs will be looking for people who have *worked for two to five years on HIV* and it will be harder to get hired for those positions. If you want to get in on the ground floor, you need to make the transition sooner, not later!"

I listened to the voices of reason, yet I postponed making an immediate decision. I started to expand my areas of interest and expertise. In the meantime, I had a meningitis outbreak in Burundi, and in the fall of 1992 I had another yellow fever outbreak, this time in Kenya. As an epidemiologist, you approach all outbreaks in a similar fashion. You answer the questions of "who, when, how, and where." Answering these questions will help you focus on the known facts and lead you to develop an hypothesis as to what is causing the outbreak.

Chapter 41

Leaving

The Western New Year had come and passed. It was now 1993, and things were calm in Addis. I was still acting director of the EPR Centre, but WHO/Geneva was actively in recruitment mode for the next director. Geneva was also looking for an officer to head up the response activities. Countries in East Africa were interested in meningitis preparedness activities and were willing to develop preparedness plans, but plans would remain just ideas on paper unless resources were found for making those plans operational.

Despite assurances that Geneva was searching for funding and resources, I thought it best to look for other programs with assured funding for their undertakings. I was looking for positions in immunizations, diarrheal prevention and control, prevention and control of malaria, and—yes—HIV/AIDS. I wanted to keep my proficiency in French, so I was looking for positions in francophone Africa with WHO, but also with USAID and nongovernmental organizations (NGOs).

Romene was growing by leaps and bounds. She was still in the ninety-eighth percentile in height and skinny (fiftieth percentile in weight). If we stayed in Ethiopia, I needed to find some type of daycare or early nursery school to put her in, so she would start to socialize and not be the center of attention all the time. I guessed I could wait to see where my next posting might be.

Sometime in March, I received word that I was selected for the post of director of a Family Health International (FHI) project on HIV/AIDS in Dakar, Senegal. FHI was a leading NGO in the fields of global health and development. Since its founding in 1971, FHI was a global leader in family planning and reproductive health, and since 1986, FHI assisted in the worldwide response to HIV/AIDS. I needed to respond as soon as possible, because they were planning a training of all new staff in Washington DC in June for an orientation to FHI, and then an orientation to the HIV project that would be my focus. I was excited, but also scared. I needed to weigh the pros and cons of the job offer. After dinner that evening, and once Romene was in bed, I asked Missah, the nanny, to make a huge fire in the living room.

I settled into my comfortable Ethiopian chair and drew a line down the middle of my yellow legal pad. One heading was "pros'" and the other was "cons." Under the pros column I listed the following: definite job offer, knowledge of the Senegalese culture, francophone country, a handful of friends still working in Dakar, and tackling a new public health emergency. The cons column, likewise, had its share of items. The biggest hurdle was taking on HIV/AIDS after consistently arguing that childhood illnesses and malaria killed more children and it was necessary to continue working on them. Another negative was that Romene would lose her Amharic language and culture, but that had always been in the cards. I was never going to live forever in Ethiopia. On the bright side, she would learn French. Realistically, no other job offer existed with the position and the funding assured. I knew what I needed to do. I would send off the acceptance email the next day.

Chapter 42

The End

There is an old African proverb that says, "*If you want to know the end, look at the beginning.*" The first time I arrived in Ethiopia, I had come on vacation from Senegal. And, three years later, I was heading back to Senegal.

Ethiopia had offered an opportunity. I worked in an African country that had never been colonized, with a rich cultural heritage, with its own language and ways of measuring time and dates. Ethiopia had once been an unknown entity. It was no longer unknown. I appreciated the rich cultural celebrations, such as the coffee ceremony. The country's national attractions, such as Simien Mountains National Park and a UNESCO World Heritage site—Lalibela—rivaled those found in the United States.

I had no inkling beforehand that I would be caught up in a civil war not of my choosing and would rescue a family in distress. In medicine, I was always trying to help alleviate suffering. Because I was working in public health and the health of the community, it was hard to see how I affected the individual. So the letter of thanks from Patricia Williams for rescuing her infant son from

Debre Zeit made a profound impact on me. One person could make a difference.

Ethiopia also gave me my daughter—Romene. I supposed, on reflection, that the explosion of the underground munitions depot prepared me in certain ways for my response to being ordered to leave the country. All during the time of the explosions, I kept looking for ways to escape the rockets and never gave up in despair or panic. It seemed perverse that I had found my daughter against all odds and then I was being ordered to leave. Since the US government could not help me, I needed to find a solution with the Ethiopian government. I had to keep focused and not panic.

As a positive person, I believed in the goodness of most people and that justice would prevail. I assumed that funding for the long-term position would come through. And it did. This tale had a happy ending. My daughter and I returned to Ethiopia, and I completed her adoption in Addis Ababa. I also completed the goals of my assignment. Ethiopia had developed a prevention and control plan, all health staff were trained in it, and it was fully operational with vaccines and medicines pre-positioned to prevent any outbreak.

I now decided I needed to take on a new challenge—HIV/AIDS—if I wanted to stay marketable in a changing demand for experts in "new" diseases. Romene would certainly grow up losing her maternal language, Amharic, but she would gain a new language, French, which in the long run would probably serve her better in being bilingual. I was apprehensive because, although I knew Senegal, I had worked in the area of vaccinations, and most parents would go to great lengths to save their children. HIV/AIDS, on the other hand, was a highly stigmatized illness due to it being a sexually transmitted disease and *it had no cure*. I realized that good was always paired with bad.

For the last month of my stay in Addis, I decided to move back into the Hilton Hotel. I had lived in Addis for almost three years, and yet I never was provided an "official lodging." I had taken a private residence and, although no money passed hands in Ethiopia, I didn't want to run afoul of the government at this late date. I had to pack up our things, and they would be airlifted from Addis. But I still had not made a crucial decision.

I was new to my next organization, and they were doing a six-week orientation in Washington DC for new staff to the HIV/AIDS projects in a number of countries around the world. It would be hard to juggle taking care of Romene solo in DC, and I decided I would try to take one of the household staff to help with Romene—whom I would leave with my parents in California. My parents were a little old to take care of a rambunctious toddler and Missah, the nanny, would be a perfect choice to accompany us—except that she spoke no English. If I was staying with my parents it wouldn't be a problem, but I was heading right off for orientation.

"Monica, what do you think if I ask Nigist to go to the States with me for about three months and take care of Romene in my parents' house?" I queried.

"You know, Connie, I think that's a great idea. She could take care of Romene, but also help your mom with the cleaning and cooking. Missah is closer to Romene, but six weeks of not being able to communicate with someone might be too stressful for your parents."

It made sense. I just wasn't sure if it made "sense" to the US government. I heard they were ferocious in not giving out visas lightly to Ethiopians! I needed to urgently discuss this with the new consular officer. Mike—the officer who had weathered the rebel invasion, responded to the underground explosion, and provided Romene with a tourist visa to the States—had transferred to a new posting. That meant I had to rehash the whole history of my life all over again. But I was encouraged. Friends told me the embassy regularly gave American diplomats visas for their nannies to visit the States during their two-to-three-month home leave visits, to help take care of the children.

The new consular officer, David, listened attentively and appeared to nod his head agreeably in response to my tale.

"Yes, we do sometimes grant a visa for extenuating circumstances, so families can have assistance during their temporary return to the States. The visa is tied to the stay of the US citizen. The domestic staff can stay in the US and work for the client, *but they must return to their country when the US citizen leaves the United States. The problem, however, is that we have been noting that Ethiopians are not leaving the US and returning to their homeland.* Are you sure your housekeeper will return to Ethiopia when you and your daughter go on to Senegal?"

"David, I need Nigist to continue with me to Senegal. Once there, it will take me about two to three weeks to find staff. Then I will pay the final settlement and put her on a plane back to Ethiopia. The US is only a stopover. I also need help with Romene going on to Senegal. Nigist will be on the plane to Dakar with me, for sure!"

He did not look convinced. He recounted several recent escapades of nannies walking out of the airport after going through Immigration with the family and getting their luggage. Or, in another case, assisting the family for the two months and then disappearing on the last night before returning to Ethiopia. I sat there with my mouth hanging open. It sounded incredible.

"That won't happen here. I have never talked about taking either Missah or Nigist to the States. It's not something they have dreamed of or were planning," I insisted.

"Send her in and we will talk to her. Do you know if she has any family or property here in Ethiopia? And here are some other criteria *you* must meet. I need to see an employee contract, the hours of work, and you have to pay the minimum wage in the US. There are no guarantees, Connie!"

"I have no idea about her personal situation, but I will send her in to speak to you," I said.

And we left it at that.

One month later, I was standing in the whirlwind that is the Addis Ababa airport departure zone. Monica was seeing us off on our next adventure. I saw that Missah, the nanny, was busy playing with Romene and trying to keep her entertained. Zemennesh, who rented me our house in Old Airport, was there with her family to see us off. Nigist, the housekeeper and cook, was looking excited and nervous in her traditional Ethiopian national dress. The US Embassy had reluctantly provided a B-1 visa for her to accompany us to the US for three months. She also agreed to go on to Senegal and help me settle in while I looked for a Senegalese housekeeper. I looked down at her feet and my heart sank. She had this suitcase that looked like it had been through the war and was bulging at the seams. Christ, that is not going to make it to the US without bursting open, I thought. I had specifically asked Nigist if she needed me to buy her a suitcase, but she had said she had one. Too late to do anything now.

"OK folks, sorry to break up the party, but we need to start going through the airport procedures," I stated authoritatively and started to push the trolley.

Everyone was crying except Romene. She was literally whirling in circles. I nonchalantly led my troop up the escalator to find our departure gate. I wondered when or if we would ever return to Ethiopia. Romene would surely want to find her roots. So this was unlikely to be the last time we would see Bole Airport! I glanced back over my shoulder and lifted my hand to wave one last goodbye. But Monica was already swallowed up in the murky currents of the crowd below.

Chapter 43

Postscript

It's been twenty-seven years since the events I describe in this book. Yet the memories are so fresh in my mind. I wrote weekly letters home to my parents, which they kept and I read many times during my home leave vacations. Unfortunately, after my mom died, I could not find the letters. I tore up the house looking for them. But all was not lost. Over the years once my daughter was able to formulate words, she loved me to tell *her* story!

"Mom, tell me how you got me out of Ethiopia during the war," was a frequent request.

Monica Wernette, Romene's godmother, who lived through those tumultuous times in Addis Ababa with me, remains a close friend and reviewed the book to make sure I kept to the facts.

After leaving Ethiopia, I was posted, in succession, to Senegal, India, and then Kenya. Romene was barely two and a half when she started learning French and Wolof (the national language of Senegal). One day she came home from kindergarten and said to me, "Mom, I know that you are American, but I'm Senegalese, right?" I shook my head and said "No! I'm American, and you're American, but you were born in Ethiopia."

When Romene was twelve, we did go back to Ethiopia from my post assignment in Nairobi to *"discover our roots."* We visited the "orphan ward" at Black Lion Hospital, but Dr. Naviat was no longer the director there. The *abuna* of St George's Cathedral was not the same one as during the war. But he called for a guard who was present during the rebel takeover. The guard remembered that he heard a baby crying, but by the time he got to the front steps the Tigrayan soldiers had snatched up the infant and were headed away. I'm not sure about the reliability of the story, but I took a photo of Romene with the guard and the *abuna*. I located the house in Old Airport where we once lived. The American diplomatic family now living there kindly let us in to see our old home. Romene remembered where her "play house" was erected in the front garden. I was also able to ultimately track down Zemennesh, who rented us the house.

In a later job from 2002 to 2011, as Regional Advisor of Infectious Diseases at the USAID Regional Office in Nairobi, Ethiopia was one of nine countries that I provided consultations to on infectious disease—particularly *TB-HIV and Avian Flu*. During the ten years I worked in Nairobi, I returned to Ethiopia many times for work. In Nairobi, Romene and I would often go for an Ethiopian meal after seeing the Sunday matinee of a movie. Unfortunately, Romene never got a chance to return one more time to Ethiopia before she left for college. Romene went to the University of Puget Sound (Tacoma, WA) and is following her dreams in Los Angeles. She visits me frequently in Mexico.

Ethiopia will forever hold a special place in my heart because, of all the things it gave me, it gave me my daughter.

About the Author

Dr. Cornelia E. Davis, better known as Connie, is an author, speaker, renowned epidemiologist and disease detective. She was sent by the World Health Organization (WHO) to Ethiopia in 1990 to help African Ministries of Health prevent or control outbreaks of meningococcal meningitis. While working in Addis Ababa, she was caught up in the fast-moving civil war and stayed behind as Acting Director of the WHO EPR Centre when UN staff were evacuated. A series of events led her to a three-month-old infant found on the steps of St. George's Cathedral. She described this exciting adventure in her new memoir, *Three Years in Ethiopia*.

Connie was raised in the San Francisco Bay Area, attended Gonzaga University, and was one of the first black women admitted to the University of California, San Francisco School of Medicine (1968). After finishing a pediatric residency, she was hired by WHO to work in the Smallpox Eradication Program in India (1975-77). This highly successful program changed her medical focus and inspired her first book, *Searching for Sitala Mata: Eradicating Smallpox in India*.

Connie earned her Masters of Public Health (MPH) degree from Johns Hopkins School of Public Health and went on to work in the EIS (Epidemic Intelligence Service) at the Centers for Disease Control in Atlanta. For the next 30 years, she battled disease outbreaks in Africa and Asia for WHO and USAID. An intrepid world traveler, she has worked in or traveled to 97 countries and territories. She lives on the northern shores of Lake Chapala near Guadalajara, Mexico.

Bring Dr. Cornelia "Connie" Davis to your Organization

Dr. Davis is available for speaking engagements. She is an award-winning author, medical consultant, speaker, traveler, and wayfarer.

Her topics include: inspirational speeches, world health issues, intercountry adoption, and traveling to remote destinations. At a recent gathering, participants said, "She took us along on a journey to places that most of us will never experience. We were all captivated and inspired by her adventures. We loved her book." And so will your audiences.

Contact information below:
Email: CorneliaEDavisMD@gmail.com
Author website: www.CorneliaEDavisMD.com

Follow Dr. Davis on Social Media

Facebook: www.Facebook.com/CorneliaEDavisMD
Pinterest: https://www.pinterest.com.mx/corneliaedavis/
Twitter: www.Twitter.com/CEDavisMD

Dear Reader, before you go, could you please place a review on Amazon about this book? There are many readers just like you, who will want to know if they would like it too.

www.ingramcontent.com/pod-product-compliance
Lightning Source LLC
Chambersburg PA
CBHW070733020526
44118CB00035B/1238